LOVING LANGUAGE

LEARNING TO HEAR YOUR NEIGHBOR

LOVING LANGUAGE

LEARNING TO HEAR YOUR NEIGHBOR

RICHARD C. BENTON, JR.

GLOSSAHOUSE
WILMORE, KY
www.glossahouse.com

Loving Language: Learning to Hear Your Neighbor

© GlossaHouse, 2022

GlossaHouse, LLC
110 Callis Circle
Wilmore, KY 40309
www.GlossaHouse.com

Benton, Richard C., Jr.
Loving Language: Learning to Hear Your Neighbor / Richard C. Benton, Jr. — Wilmore, KY: GlossaHouse © 2022

      x, 175p. 15.24cm. —

      ISBN-13: 978-1-63663-0410

      Library of Congress Control Number: 2022920427

Corrected December 9, 2022

Cover design by T. Michael W. Halcomb

Text layout by Fredrick J. Long

The fonts used to create this work are available from
www.linguistsoftware.com/lgku.htm

To Dr. Thomas Coates, who taught me
at 13 that my mouth can speak any language

TABLE OF CONTENTS

PART I
LOVING LANGUAGE

INTRODUCTION

"Those stupid do-gooders!" my friend's dad, Carl, sneered. I was at my friend's house, and his father brought up a conversation at his church. "They want to start up English classes for foreigners." Since this was Denver, the population included many Spanish-speakers with minimal command of English. "I told them, 'Look, they actually don't want to learn English. They'd rather speak Spanish.'" He narrowed his eyes at his imagined audience, "'If you want to do them a favor, hire a teacher, sit your butts in the seats and learn Spanish!'"

Carl spoke Spanish fluently. He studied in Spain when he was in college, married an Argentine, and worked at a job where he needed to enter people's homes. Working hard to learn Spanish simplified explaining the reasons why an unfamiliar White man might ask to look around the house of a Hispanic family. Every week, his Spanish allowed him to work and connect with people at work and beyond.

He also understood what these people might not have understood: learning a language is hard. Speaking your native language is easy. Learning Spanish not only teaches you a new language, but the process teaches empathy for other people trying to learn any new language later in life.

The mistake of Carl's do-gooder fellow-parishioners surely does not look like a mistake at first glance. If you come to the US, you must learn English. A good deed would, therefore, be to offer to help in such a pursuit.

Yet, the statement reveals too many assumptions. No such universal truth exists that one must learn the language of the country one moves to. (Take the British Empire, for example!) Nothing but the mentality of native-born Americans requires learning English, but that notion only arises because Americans assume that anglophones do not have to learn another language. Americans, according to the cliché, are bad at languages; however, they believe that anyone coming to this country will learn English unless they deliberately choose not to. They believe that when others learn English, being "bad at languages" should not be an excuse.

Blind to this assumption, they do not see the suffering that it causes. They do not see the humiliation of parents in front of their children at the hands of teachers, police, or healthcare workers—whether accidental or malicious. Such people must choose whether to rest after work or go to class and do homework. And some watch their children slip away from them as English crowds out the "mother tongue" that they grew up speaking.

They do not see the terror that brought us to this point, where generation after generation of politicians and citizens believed that speakers of other languages endangered themselves and our society at large. The great-grandparents of these monolingual anglophones supposedly "picked up" English in a gauzy history because they were different than today's supposedly lazy, rebellious immigrants.

The liberal wants to teach the immigrant English; the conservative wants them to pick it up without help. Neither—having recently or long ago forgotten the language of their ancestors—wants to learn the language of the immigrant. "The challenges of the past and the burden of forgetting," Lonnie G. Bunch of the Smithsonian Institution wrote, "weighs heavily on a nation's subconscious."[1] As in every wave of immigration, becoming American means to forget.

❦

This book proposes a way for Americans to right the wrongs perpetrated upon their ancestors: other than the small population descended from pure English stock, this country destroyed the language that

---

[1] Lonnie Bunch, "Black History Matters to Everyone—It's a Crucial Part of Our Nations' Story," *The Guardian*, October 31, 2018.

connected us to our ancestors. We see it happening still—and on our watch. It would seem that languages come to the US to die.

A huge number of languages are spoken in the US: 430 according to Wikipedia.[2] When I shop at the store, when I sit in the public library, when I go to work, I may hear another language besides English a few times per month. Despite how many languages are spoken at *home*, few are spoken in *public*.

We can help change this troubling strain of American culture. If we want to turn the tide on language loss—not just Native American languages, but also on all the old-world ones—we must bring out languages into the public sphere. All of us will have to work so that English does not crowd them out, and so we will strive to make space.

In order to create this capacity for languages other than English, we must begin with our own mind. If English takes all the space in our brain, it will inevitably infest every space we enter. Conversely, if only English exists in our minds, English will persist everywhere we go. As kindly as we might look upon other languages, the words that come out of our mouths will take all the space. I have seen this happen with Americans everywhere from Hawaii to Kyiv, let alone the US mainland.

For our culture to enjoy multiple languages, we ourselves must be multilingual. We must learn other languages. Our children must live among multiple languages. Before our immigrant or indigenous neighbor opens their mouth, we must invite their language in.

Once languages have the home in the US that we claim to offer to all-comers in the world, we will see what wisdom, knowledge, and experience have been locked away in those "foreign" words. More solutions, more dialogue, better business will result.

---

[2] "Languages of the United States," in *Wikipedia*, Oct 23, 2021, https://en.wikipedia.org/w/index.php?title=Languages_of_the_United_States&oldid=1051411593.

Moreover, as we stumble through learning them, once our "butts are in the chairs," we will be transformed. We will be serving our neighbors, those who have left their homes and families and communities— "the foreigners in our midst." We will embarrass ourselves, making ourselves vulnerable for the sake of others. One day, our multilingual America can hear the voices of all those in the world through the concrete work, effort, and red-faced embarrassment of speaking a language badly. When the native-born accept the vulnerable situation of the immigrant, the society of the US can become open and welcoming and wise.

Read further for the ultimate cure for monolingualism....

This book unfolds in four parts. In part one, it describes my personal love of languages that brought me to see the role that language plays in people's lives. My language-love centered first on travel abroad and then on relationships with my neighbors. From that transformation, I describe how to observe and really listen to the languages in one's own linguistic environment, which I will define as "ecolinguism."

Part two follows the path of power that created a famously monolingual country from the hundreds of languages that have been spoken here. From a specific story of language elimination (Swiss German) to broader narratives about a society that hobbled and destroyed languages of indigenous, enslaved, and immigrant people, we will see the official positions and policies that raised "national security" above the well-being of citizens, simply because of the languages they spoke. Sadly, the section will also reveal how such violence continues to the present day.

Part three turns the tables. When connections and relationships with people different from us guide us, we can start to act decisively through learning languages—if only a few words. This section will also offer examples from various spheres of life (schools, government, religious) where institutions have created ways for our citizens to become speakers of other languages. From these seeds can sprout a healthier "ecolinguistic sphere." We could live in a truly remarkable society that values these languages—which seem presently to annoy and cause friction—for the wisdom and experience they communicate and share with all of us who have ears to hear.

Finally, in part four, the reader will learn the invaluable state of vulnerability that opens them to a braver, more wholehearted life, while connecting them to others. Vulnerability springs forth eternally from speaking other languages because of the challenges and embarrassments the learning process requires. This section ought to encourage the reader to make many mistakes rather than speak perfectly. There is no better time to start than the present—and the less you know, the easier it will be to make those golden mistakes.

Learning languages does not simply result in knowing something new, like black holes or geometry, but in the ability to become a more open person, more connected to others, through concrete action. Ultimately, you can learn your neighbor's language, so that the next generation will remember and teach their children. Our country can live with rich linguistic connections, spoken by caring, hardworking neighbors.

CHAPTER 1

FRIENDS ABROAD

Gift

"Bellati minute wahdah!" "Wait a minute!" said Mustafa in his local Arabic dialect with his hand raised.

I am standing on the street in Marrakech, Morocco, with a friend of mine, nervous about what he wants us to wait for. After living there for six months, I received a visit from my parents, whom I introduced to my friends. I am worried the situation might get awkward.

My trip to Morocco began during my last weeks as a college student in Kyiv, Ukraine, where I made friends with a pair of Moroccan roommates. When I told them I wanted to live abroad to study a language for a year after university, they invited me to their homeland. One of them even offered to find me a place to stay through his family members.

Language and adventure motivated my visit; I wanted to see how far I could push my learning abilities. Starting with two Arabic words, how well could I speak after nine months of immersion?

My friend's brother-in-law worked at a bank, so with little else to do, I visited him regularly, and thanks to those visits I made friends with Alaa. Alaa ran a bicycle-parking service outside the bank. Rather than carry bike locks, cyclists in Marrakech at that time counted on businesses, which often employed a *guardien* who watched bicycles and mopeds for a small tip. Alaa watched the bikes, so he sat there all day, gossiping with passers-by, reading papers from the news kiosk on his corner, and observing people. He was one of my most important Arabic teachers.

During my days with Alaa, he not only bore my language with infinite patience, but he told me jokes, taught me local slang, and helped me to read. Visits to the bank always included a language lesson. I would drop by and sit on a bench next to him for one or even two hours before moving on.

As I spent time with Alaa, a lot of folks would teach me, too. One was Mustafa. As far as I could tell, he was a hustler and a beggar. Even though he was in his early twenties, surely not much older than I was, his face was creased from the sun and cigarettes. He was never alone, as he always pushed the wheelchair of his brother, who was severely disabled and unable to speak. The pair would often peel away from chatting with us to go hit up some tourists for change before coming back. Mustafa's main pedagogical material for me consisted of dirty jokes, which he relished explaining to this naïve foreigner, and which I only knew were dirty when Alaa cut him off.

I did not know about Mustafa's plan upon seeing my parents. My middle-class, White family precisely fit his profile of a mark. I felt uneasy that he might hit up my parents for change, but I did not want to insult him. We waited for him and his brother to return.

A few minutes later he returned and brought his hand out from behind his back: a rose, presented to my mother. When we offered to give him some money for it, he refused. He only expressed his honor in welcoming my parents and wished them a wonderful stay in his country.

Travelers

"Do you speak English?" I asked. The weary man shook his head *No* and pointed to the young woman sitting next to him.

Hearing him speak a language I could not identify, I did not immediately accept his answer but kept going. "What language were you speaking?" I asked. "Kurdish," he managed to answer.

"Where are you from?" I asked, again in English.

"Syria," he answered.

"Ah! *Anta bithaki al-arabiy kaman?*" "Do you speak Arabic, too?"

9

"*Aywah,*" "Yes," he answered slowly with a smile.

Locals warned me that the only way to travel from Athens to Thessaloniki, Greece's second-biggest city, was by plane. I took my younger daughter on a trip there when she turned 13, and my mother—terminally infected with wanderlust—accompanied us. So that they could see the countryside from the ground level, I decided we would ignore the advice of locals and take the train.

On boarding, I noticed that the travelers were not vacationers. Most wore older clothes, a little shabby and not particularly stylish. They carried cardboard boxes in cheap plastic bags instead of luggage. Outside of the tourist bubble I was used to, their poverty felt menacing, I am embarrassed to admit. A voice in my head reminded me to keep an eye on our bags.

Across from us sat a family with an olive complexion—not uncommon in this part of the world; my family looked much more out-of-place than they did. A man and a woman appeared to be in their 60s, and a younger pair, in their 20s or early 30s. Their faces looked too tired to sleep as they spoke quietly or stared silently out the window in turn.

They were speaking a language I could not recognize—not a single word. My Greek is not good, so maybe some dialect? When a woman pushed a sandwich cart by, she addressed them in English, not Greek; they had to be foreign. My own family recognized the look on my face as I was drawn into their conversation. *Romanian?* No, I would have grasped a couple words. *Albanian?* Could be, since lots resided in the country. *Roma?* I was hoping, but it was unlikely.

I could no longer hold back, so I asked and received the reply: "Kurdish."

It was June 2015, six months before the tragic death of Alan Kurdi, a little boy who drowned in the Mediterranean and whose photo awoke the world to the desperate families fleeing across the Sea. At this point, I had only heard whispers about this great refugee migration.

"I've been to Syria," I continued in Arabic. "I visited the Sednaya Monastery." I spent a day at this unique, 1400-year-old site a few years ago, in 2010, shortly before the civil war began.

"Really? I worked at Sednaya!"

Even though my Arabic was not great (the Syrian dialect is very different from the Moroccan one), we reminisced about better days in Syria. We talked about days when Kurd, Sunni Arab, and Orthodox Christian lived and worked together peacefully, when a Westerner like me could freely travel around the country. I learned about his wife and children, whom he left at the Turkish side of the border with Syria, and his parents who, as the eldest in the family, volunteered to stay behind in their home to protect what they could for the rest of the family.

After several hours, we finally arrived at Thessaloniki. We were getting off. As I stood, my new friend's uncle stood up and shook my hand. He smiled and in Arabic said, "Thank you! Very nice to meet you!"

"Allah khaleekum!" "May God preserve you!" I answered.

Breaking Bread

"How can you treat a foreigner like that? You can see he can't understand you!"

My hackles were up, but I could not form the right Russian words to speak up for myself. I was riding the trolley with one of my university classmates in Kyiv, Ukraine, and felt grateful when this woman sitting next to us raised her voice.

"Ma'am, this is really none of your business," my classmate deflected.

"It's none of your business to talk that way!"

The girl I was with muttered a response and stopped bickering.

I arrived in Ukraine in 1993, two years after the fall of the Soviet Union. Up till then, Westerners were rare, and Americans, more so. Everyone had seen them in movies, but rarely walking the streets of Kyiv. I had landed in a university class of 17- and 18-years-olds girls, many of whom came from smaller towns and for whom the capital itself was a novelty. As a flesh-and-blood manifestation of American culture in their classroom, I created a stir.

Spending time with the only American and only boy in the class became a premium, and jealousy arose, which was likely the reason for the bad scene on the trolley. Some in my class simply did not know how to interact with a foreigner, such as this one who was making fun at my expense. After a few months I could carry on a conversation in Russian and, to a lesser extent, in Ukrainian, but I could not defend myself well from verbal attack. I was a rare bird, and a talking one at that; some treated—and other abused—me like a pet.

Strangers would come up to me to talk. Someone had told them about me, and they wanted to see if it / I was true. One girl was so nervous when I asked her a question, she jumped when I said her name to ask her a question. One boy would follow me everywhere—even into the bathroom—so he could try out speaking English. A couple times, I visited friends' houses, and they told their moms to talk to me and not to stare.

Since I learned the local languages, they told me stories. No one I knew could afford restaurants, so we spent hours eating at someone's home, which I discovered later cost them the equivalent for me of several hundred dollars. The mother of my host mother told me about working at a bread factory in the 1940s, the best job after World War II, after the Nazis withdrew from a devastated Ukraine. My friend's father told me about the best coat for working in an oil field in Siberia. A local painter took me around to his friends at an arts festival, and they all had a piece to show and explain to me. Local poets came to my host family's house, and they recounted with devotion the history and resiliency of the Ukrainian language. A Protestant pastor described stories both funny and sad of life as a believer under the Communist regime. Many related to the hyperinflation they were experiencing and repeated the same dark joke, "In Soviet times we all dreamed of being millionaires, and now we are all millionaires! We have to be one just to buy a kilo of sausage!"

While I was the exotic one, once I learned the language, the people taught me—about bread: the most important job. The reason for back-breaking work. Love of language and God, which transcended food. The struggle to buy bread in an economy destroyed.

The honor of breaking bread with a foreigner at your table, because that is how you treat guests, even if it costs a week's salary.

Speak to Hear

Interactions with strangers have deepened my understanding of the world. Different from the standard tourist, I met and spent time with people who were invisible to others: the bike guardian, the beggar, the refugee, the family at their home dinner table.

They continuously flipped my expectations. The patience of the well-read menial laborer, the generosity of the beggar, the resilience of the refugee in flight all taught me that I cannot understand someone until I know their story.

Many years ago, I was trying to think what to call the movement I wanted to wish into existence, to speak into being, where I wanted to encourage people to learn languages in order to make connections with people otherwise separate from us, whose stories we could not know without a means of communication. My friend suggested, "Speak to Hear." That is, by learning how to *speak* their language, we could *hear* their story.

Speaking and hearing led to a heartfelt connection. My desire to learn the language motivated gifts, smiles, and precious time and patience to teach me more.

Sometimes I feel like a colonizer, as if I swooped into a country with more money and mobility than anyone around me. I learned the language because of enjoyment and took advantage of my wealth and leisure to extract knowledge from the "natives" of the land I was visiting.

The generosity shown to me, in fact, put me to shame. They forced me to look at how I lived in my own country. When did I ever offer a gift—

even a small one—to a stranger? How much time do I offer to someone who is struggling with my language? When did I thank someone from my heart, just for listening to the difficult parts of my story?

When I travel now, I always learn some of the language(s) I might run across, no matter how "useful" afterwards. I learned a handful of Basque words when visiting our former exchange student in Northern Spain and took some Macedonian lessons for when I visited my daughter in Skopje. On the one hand, I craved the surprising connections I could make. On the other hand, the hard work of learning signaled to others that I am making a sincere effort to connect.

Making the effort differs from the desire to learn the language. I taught a summer-intensive course in Biblical Hebrew in Ukraine. I began with nine students. By the end of the first day, I had eight, and so it went until I had four solid students after the first week. The collapse of attendance led me to apologize to our department chair. She shook her head, "Don't worry. Look, many people desire to *know* Hebrew, but not many want to *learn* Hebrew." If I want to connect with the people I meet when I travel, practicing the language is the best way to signal that I want to learn and to connect in a real way.

As divisions between "us" and "them," "Americans" and "immigrants," "insiders" and "outsiders" gape, we can do something to bridge them. Learning to speak the language of the other affords us an action to hear and to love them.

CHAPTER 2
MY AIRPORT FRIENDS

Bringing Lessons Home

Languages provided connections and stories. When I entered a new environment, languages allowed me to view the world differently. My kind of "vacation" could transform me in ways that sightseeing alone does not allow.

Coming back home to the US, I began to see my community in new ways. People had come from other countries here, to my home, speaking their languages. They bore the very stories and connections to their homelands that moved me when I was abroad.

Living abroad for long periods offered me energy and joy, but became more of a burden as my family grew. I hoped my children could connect with a land, a place, and its people to find a home in a community. As a result, my wife and I looked for a place where we could set down roots for the sake of our daughters. Travel became shorter and rarer.

To my unexpected pleasure, these people around me offered me the energy my curiosity thirsted for. Connecting with them satiated my wanderlust without needing to travel. I sought a way to connect, to learn languages, and to experience more of the world without an airplane, simply by going for a cup of coffee. Significantly, many of my conversations took place in the liminal spaces between the US and abroad: airports.

A Three-by-five-inch Doorway

On one trip, I saw a young worker at the Denver airport walking towards me. Maybe he was Ethiopian? I stepped in front of him, smiled, and looked him in the eye. *"Dehna neh?"* ("Are you good?") I asked.

"You speak Amharic?" he asked with a wide smile and raised eyebrows. "Well…" I could not very well respond "yes," since my entire Amharic knowledge literally fit in the size of my hand.

This conversation began a week before, in another airport. During a layover at the Minneapolis airport, I had seen an older gentleman seated in a uniform talking on the phone. He looked East African. "Excuse me. I like to study languages. Can I ask you what language you were speaking?"

"Amharic."

"Would you mind telling me how to say a few things in your language?"

"What would you like to know?"

"How do you say, 'Hello!'" I pulled out a pen and three-by-five-inch notecard from my pocket.

He was friendly and open, so the conversation unfolded. I collected "How are you?" and "Are you Ethiopian?" scratched out phonetically as best as I could without a real surface to write on. I found out that I had to write out these phrases a few times: each was pronounced differently depending if speaking to a man or a woman.

When the young man approached me in the Denver airport, I was prepared. I took my notes from Minneapolis that I had practiced and encountered a potential test. When I opened my mouth to speak, it worked. Amharic connected me to him.

My new friend invited me, in spite of my lame answer, to meet his colleagues, who included not only Ethiopians but also a Moroccan man and a Sudanese woman. I spent the rest of my layover standing at the end of the concourse getting to know the wheelchair-pushers as I was an invited guest among those whom I had, to my shame, never noticed before.

The Risk of Adventure

When you see this episode from the outside, it might look easy for someone else (some "language person" or "polyglot" or "gifted person") but unimaginable for you. But here is the secret: speaking a new language risks humiliation for everyone. Looking like an adult, I sound like a child. I have to ignore the butterflies in my stomach every time to make the above interactions happen, one single word at a time. My next move was clear, but my inner gremlins distracted me with protecting my ego.

Phase 1: I had to ask for the phrase.

I'm not sure if they'll appreciate being interrupted. Are they actually on break? Will I sound annoying? Selfish? Suspicious? I mean, no one does this! If they don't understand me, this will be a big waste of time. If I don't understand them, it will be completely humiliating. A combination might result in a terrible back-and-forth of "What?" "What?" "What did you say?" "Sorry." "I don't understand." "I'm sorry I bothered you."

I took the risk in Minneapolis. They taught me their words. We smiled and connected.

Phase 2: I had to speak.

Putting my knew "knowledge" on the line in Denver disheartened me, in fact. Several days had passed between my outbound flight in Minneapolis when I had heard those words spoken and the return. I had to rely on the unverified "transcription" I had scratched onto my paper.

> *What if I can't read my own notes? What if I wasted the time of that first gentleman? What if my words are completely incomprehensible to this man? He might give me a puzzled look and ask me to repeat myself. Even worse, he could miss me entirely and walk right by because I'm speaking gibberish, for all he knows.*

In addition to quieting my anxious psyche, I had to overcome natural barriers. I had to speak loudly enough for him to hear. He had to notice me, too. Amharic words unexpectedly coming out of a white face usually catch native speakers off guard. By looking him in the eye and catching his attention, I wanted him to hear precisely what I was trying to say.

I spoke his language, and he heard. We saw each other.

Missteps and Grace

Another year and at another airport—this time in Seattle—a man walked by, and his face looked East African to me. *"Dehna ne?"* I smiled. I was excited to try out my Amharic again.

"Dehna negn!" he grinned back. It felt so nice to make a connection, and he reacted positively to me. I was still chasing that time I spent with those Denver "friends."

"You're from Ethiopia?" I continued in English.

He smiled. "No, I'm from Somalia."

I spoke the wrong language! My stomach plummeted. I was fortunate that he had learned enough Amharic—a totally foreign language for him—to allow me to save face.

My line continued to move, and he had to continue to work. "Uh...nice to meet you," I stammered, humiliated.

From the heart, he responded, "Nice to meet you, too!"

Washing off the stink of shame took me a couple days. *Man, I looked dumb! I was so overconfident that I didn't even think to ask him where he was from before I showed off!* My confidence went down the tubes as I felt like an ignorant, White colonist.

Then I stopped to think of what I actually saw. This young man's expression did not express "dumb, White American." He truly looked amused, even happy. I did not see my shame register with him. We may actually have connected. I struggled to bring together my shame with his delight. Too embarrassed to notice, it later struck me that he learned as much Amharic as I had; we shared something in common.

In the end, I had to admit: if I am going to try this whole East African language "project," I will blunder, maybe even worse than this. I know I want to connect with others, but I also know that I will not always come off "cool." If I want to speak to them in their language, I will fail—but I will not stop, because I may still make a connection with him. I cannot let my shame prevent me from connecting.

Spending Time Making Friends

Having checked into my flight at the Minneapolis airport many years later, I was frustrated second-guessing myself over which security line would be faster. It takes ten minutes to walk to one from the other, so once you choose, you are committed. A twenty-minute return walk offers no benefit. I had to choose wisely.

You know who knows the situation better than anyone? The folks who work there.

By this point, ten years had passed, and I had moved to the Twin Cities of Minnesota. I once again found myself in the Minneapolis airport. The extensive East African community welcomed me with as much heart as my young friend in Denver.

I saw a pair of gentlemen wearing Delta uniforms, standing at the side of the crowd. "What might they be?" I asked myself. "Ethiopian?"

I tried Amharic. *"Dehna nesh!"* ("Are you good?") I had memorized my notecard by now.

My word was met by a puzzled look.

Oops! I used the greeting you use for addressing a woman. "I'm sorry...*Dehna neh!"*

"Dehna negn!" ("I'm good!") he grinned. "You speak my language?"

"Uh...*tenish tenish"* ("a little bit").

Over the intervening years, I met many Amharic speakers. The coworker who introduced me to this phrase *"tenish tenish"* confided, "If you say this, Ethiopians won't speak Amharic around you because they'll be afraid you might understand them." My friends taught me enough to be dangerous—or to appear to be, at least.

"Ah! *Tenish tenish,*" both men nodded.

"Which security line is fastest?"

"Where is your gate?"

"I just want to get through fast."

"Ah! Well, on that end," he pointed left, "the line is long. But on that side," indicating the other direction, "they have more lines open."

"*Ahmesugenalew!*" I thanked him and started walking away.

"Have you been to Ethiopia?" he asked, enticing me to turn back. He was obviously less interested in my speedy passage through security than I was.

"No, but I hope to one day."

"How do you know my language?"

"From my friends. And from the airport."

"Really? Your friends teach you?" one said.

"Yes," I grinned. "*Ahmesugenalew!*" I thanked him again as I tried to continue on. "*Salamne!*" ("Peace!")

"*Salamne dehna hun!*" he answered.

I stopped and turned back. (They were making it so hard to leave.) "...*dehna hun?* What does that mean?"

"It means, 'Good bye!'" he said. The other added with his own smile, "Now you have new friends!"

We shook hands as I moved towards the security line. My new friends finally made me forget that I wanted to save time.

Guiding the Lost

I continued to the security area those gentlemen suggested.

"Can I help you?" the agent at the line asks. The multiplication of new queues has been frustrating me these days, and my face must have shown it.

"I can never figure out where to enter."

"I can help you! Show me your boarding pass." *Another Ethiopian? I wondered.*

"Oh…I think I see I'm in 'All Passengers.' Never mind," I say as I head down "my" line. *"Ahmesugenalew!"* I toss over my shoulder, just to test my internal question.

"You're wel…what? *Ahmesugenalew!* You know my language!" Ignoring the young woman behind me in line, he walked over to me and grabbed my hand. He pulled me in, and we touched shoulders in a typically Ethiopian combination hug-handshake shoulder-bump.

We traded a *"salamne"* as I restarted my walk down the security line. Even the young White woman behind me was smiling.

Before the first 15 minutes at the airport, I came with three words. I left with four words, three new friends, and a happy bystander.

The Risk Does Not End

Reflecting on the more recent Minnesota conversations, I can see momentum building. I said my handful of words enough over the years that I do not get the same butterflies I used to. At least, experience minimized their flutter, except…

Why did he look at me like that? Was I speaking nonsense? What if this isn't their language? What if they think I'm being too forward? I don't actually know them, so they might not appreciate the interruption. What if I say something wrong that could insult them?

I still manage to mess up, though not in a way that even my very imaginative fear had foreseen. Pleasant connections, in spite of or because of my language mistakes, made me feel safer. Reality did not live up to my fears in the past.

- Using the wrong gender to someone could insult them unintentionally. *They did not care.*
- Grammatically, I should have used the plural instead of the singular. *They did not mention it.*
- Just like with the Somali in Seattle, Amharic might not have been their language, as the airport employs folks who come from many ethnic groups from the Horn of Africa. Even if the language was not theirs, *they acted like it was*, just for the sake of conversation.

Then they called me their friend. I guess that is how much of life goes: the things we are afraid of do not come to pass, and the things that come to pass we have not thought of.

"Oh, look! There's one of your friends!" teases one of my teenage daughters when an East African man walks by at the airport. Such events occur often enough that my kids like to razz me about my "friends" at the airport. "Don't you know him?" she jokes. "You should say 'hello'!" My kids know how much I love to talk with these folks—and to see their delight and surprise when I speak even three words of their language.

They get it back, though. "Why you no speak Oromo?" the owner of my favorite restaurant, like an aunt, scolds my oldest child. "Your dad don't teach you?" My surprised daughter receives a playful smack in the arm.

Truly I feel I have new friends. They have worked harder to keep the conversation going than I did—even with my daughter. This outcome is at least as common as my mistakes. In spite of the fears I thought of and those that actually happened, I make friends. Accuracy does not determine how well an interaction goes, in fact. When my language comes out completely garbled, people still smile and enjoy the interaction—sometimes even more than I do.

CHAPTER 3
ECOLINGUISM

Connecting by Sharing Burdens

In school I became fascinated with languages. The patterns among tongue-twisting sounds, categories, redundancies, and superfluous grammatical intricacies would not let me turn away. Immersing myself overseas made me fall head-over-heels in love with languages as mastery of those crazy-making systems inexplicably yet predictably brought me closer to other human beings. Once I arrived back at home, I continued to follow this love. Loving language took on a more profound meaning once I realized how much I had in common with the immigrants around me in the US.

As I met speakers of other languages in my city, they taught me about the vulnerabilities they face down daily. Tasks I took no thought of, such as etiquette at work or with a cashier, could lead them to stress, humiliation, and mutual frustration. This daily struggle often left them exhausted in the short term, but over time these experiences often built up into amazing resiliency. Leaving their own linguistic micro-sphere took courage, which made them strong.

My life abroad allowed me to identify with aspects of their situation. As a student, the stress of finding my class and just knowing what classes I was taking, and as a teacher, expressing the ideas I was paid to explain, posed huge problems that those right next to me could not even see. I experienced unpleasant squints at my jokes, helplessness before bureaucrats, and a brain exercised to exhaustion by 7:00 pm. Granted, I had the privilege of wealth (in US dollars), education, and a US passport, yet I have been bullied even while the other person thought they were just joking around. I did not possess normal verbal defense-mechanisms; banter felt like a beating.

The kindness of strangers allowed me to survive when I was abroad; the privilege I brought with me, my foreignness often undermined. I could either speak English to people, by which I doubled down on foreignness and privilege, guaranteeing that I would not connect as deeply, or speak their language, where I would give up some privilege and sound a little less foreign. The struggles of the immigrants in my community who were forced into the latter situation struck a chord with me, and I wanted to offer to share their burden.

While they walked around verbally vulnerable among the local population, I, a local, wanted to make myself vulnerable for their sake. I wanted to make myself the student, the beginner, a "foreigner" to their "native," so they could rest and communicate in a way that made them feel at ease. Only after living through a period of vulnerability could I see that same vulnerability in my community, and the experience brought together multiple parts of my life. "Loving language" not only expressed my joy in learning language, but also the love towards others that learning their language exhibits.

When I found a job where I could control my own schedule, I started volunteering with refugees and writing a blog about my language love and my linguistic community. My experience moving and changing careers also brought me closer to the marginalized around me.

Foreigners made me feel at home. Language had always connected me to other countries, but now it formed relationships with my neighbors in the US. I moved to Minnesota never having lived there previously. No longer living overseas challenged my self-perception as a worldly person, but the people I met back here brought me into their world inside a land I considered my turf. Somali colleagues at my new job and an Oromo teacher who was working to increase literacy in his community—all who had lived in Minnesota longer than I had—opened themselves to me, so I began to feel part of this new community I had moved to. We shared something in common: the dissonance of never feeling completely at home in the US or elsewhere. The more I spent time with them, the more I learned; the more I discovered, the more curious I became. These phases of my life and these special people made me see my community in a new way, as a source of fascination that I had been missing by not traveling.

People in my community recognized my learning their languages as effort I put into hearing them more deeply. As I recounted in the last two chapters, strangers and friends reacted with disarming warmth on so many occasions at home and abroad that I cannot see it as a coincidence. You, too, when you go out in public, are likely surrounded by people who would welcome you to join them in their world by speaking their language.

Ecolinguism: Linguistic Ecology

To enter this world, we start asking questions. What languages are spoken in your community? Who speaks them where? How do they interact with each other? The answers to these questions describe the local linguistic environment you live in. As an analogue to ecology, I call the study of the linguistic environment, "ecolinguism."

Ecology is "the branch of biology which studies the interactions among organisms and their environment."[3] Ecologists, then, study four aspects of these interactions: 1) the life processes, interactions, and adaptations; 2) the movement of materials and energy through living communities; 3) the successional development of ecosystems; and 4) the abundance and distribution of organisms and biodiversity in the context of the environment. This covers all of the interactions of various species: how they adapt to each other by helping and preying on each other, how they distribute energy through food and thrive in different niches. And these relationships never stabilize but are always shifting.

We can study languages in a community in a similar way. "Ecolinguism," as a parallel to ecology, is *the study of the interactions among language communities and their environment*. Therefore, as we move through the different languages in our community, we can observe each one as a distinct community artifact, occupying different levels

---

[3] "Ecology," in *Wikipedia*, July 2, 2019, https://en.wikipedia.org/w/index.php?title=Ecology&oldid=904497681.

of prestige with respect to other languages and spoken in particular social spaces, both in public and at home. All of these aspects change over time.

An important assumption underlies this definition. Ecolinguism focuses on language *communities*, not individual *speakers*, just as an ecologist looks at the population of a species, not any individual member. No one learns or uses a language by themselves; hence, a language requires at least two individuals. Acquiring a language on an app by yourself is not learning a language, but you can become a speaker as soon as you interact with speakers of that language. Communities speak languages, not individuals.

We begin our ecolinguistic study by asking the questions what languages are spoken around us, where and by whom they are spoken, and how they interact with other languages. We can observe multiple languages and their sometimes-surprising relations to one another in different social settings—our local "linguasphere."

1. What Languages?

When I was traveling in Europe, local people poked fun at me, the American, with the famous joke:

> What do you call someone who knows three languages?
>
> *Trilingual.*

> What do you call someone who knows two languages?
>
> *Bilingual.*

> What do you call someone who knows one language?
>
> *American.*

We laughed because it is true—or is it? This joke assumes a single profile of "American" among an actual multitude of different backgrounds. The US is full of multilingual people. Just listen for someone with an accent! Like in ecology, we observe in our towns and neighborhoods the "abundance and distribution of [languages and linguistic diversity] in the context of the [linguistic] environment."

According to census data, in fact, roughly 1 in 5 people in the US counters the "American" described in the joke. Not only is a substantial number of Americans multilingual, the variety of languages one finds is astounding. Most citizens of Switzerland are multilingual, but those languages represent languages from a 100-mile radius: the official languages of German, French, Italian, and Romansh.[4] The US includes languages from all over the world, for example, over a million speakers each of Spanish, French, and German, as well as of several East Asian languages—Chinese languages (e.g., Mandarin, Cantonese), Tagalog, Vietnamese, and Korean.[5]

Just as you see multitudes of living things by peeking under a log in the forest, you can find other languages just by turning your gaze to the people in your everyday life. The grocery store, the community college catalog, coworkers, the families of my kids' friends, and the public library, for example, allowed me to scratch the linguistic surface of my little suburb in the Midwest US.

You can find languages unique to the US, too. In addition to Native American languages, one can hear exemples of languages that are even minorities in their native countries. At a language conference in 2015, Daniel Kaufman, a linguist of the Endangered Language Alliance who lives in New York City and works on Central American languages, recounted a conversation with a waiter in a Mexican restaurant. Kaufman had been focusing on indigenous languages of Southern Mexico, so he asked if the gentleman knew anyone in New

---

[4] Immigrants bring other languages to Switzerland. For example, about 250,000 residents speak Portuguese—roughly six times the population who speak Romansh and half the population who speaks Italian ("Languages of Switzerland," in *Wikipedia*, September 11, 2019, https://en.wikipedia.org/w/index.php?title=Languages_of_Switzerland&oldid=915147707).

[5] "The Most Spoken Languages In America," *WorldAtlas*, accessed July 1, 2019, https://www.worldatlas.com/articles/the-most-spoken-languages-in-america.html.

York who spoke one of them. "I speak one," responded the waiter. Surprised at the quick success of his inquiry, Kaufman asked himself if he was simply lucky, or if Mexican languages were more common in this city than he previously thought. It was the latter. He learned that the last speakers of some of these languages left their homes and the dwindling community now lived in New York.

When you are out and about in your community, you can ask what languages people speak. I know that some monolingual English-speakers are worried about offending someone, but I have so rarely upset anyone by asking that I no longer worry about it. (I have been yelled at by random passers-by in the street for no reason more often than someone has expressed any kind of discomfort in my questions.) One can take different approaches to asking. The most direct approach is, "What language were you just speaking?" or more obliquely you can make a wild guess, "Were you speaking Arabic (or whatever language you thought it was)?" If you are wrong, the person will likely simply correct you. Other times, I will ask in a more neutral way, "Do you speak another language besides English?" That way, I recognize their ability to speak English, while still learning what I am curious about. The added advantage comes when I find out that they speak multiple languages besides the one they were just speaking.

Sometimes I hear a familiar accent in English and I wonder where it comes from. I might just guess more directly and say, for example, *Vy govorite po-russki?* "Do you speak Russian?" On the light-rail train in Minneapolis, I overheard a man speaking with an accent with his anglophone friends. He reminded me of my Serbian friends, so I went out on a limb: *Dobar dan! Kako ste?* "Hi! How are you?" He was indeed from former Yugoslavia! As I recounted above, when I wanted to learn some Amharic at the airport, I contextualized my curiosity, "I love learning other languages, so I was wondering if you might have a few minutes to teach me a couple words in your language." If I know their language, I might break the ice by saying, "Oh! Do you speak (Spanish)? I love speaking (Spanish)!" An open heart and gratitude go a long way to staving off potential, though very unlikely, offense.

This is the attitude I take when I go out in public. When I walk through the suburban grocery store by my house, I listen for the languages being spoken. If I do not know what language a person might be speaking, I might ask. I have been known to ask people about international-looking bumper-stickers in the supermarket parking lot. When I used to work in New York City, I tried to recognize Russians in the crowd based on their facial features and expression. I would test myself by making eye contact, nodding, and saying, *Privet!* "Hello!"

Corners of the world have revealed themselves to me. I have put a lot of time into learning the Ethiopian language of Oromo, so I learned that the Twin Cities hosts the largest Oromo diaspora community in the world, such that the Prime Minister of Ethiopia makes it a point to visit our state when he comes to the US. As a result, the world Oromo community considers the Twin Cities to be an important center for their language (much to my good fortune).

My community revealed to me Indian languages. Through one of my daughters, I met a couple from Hyderabad, India, whose mother-tongue is Telugu, but who also speak Hindi, Urdu, and can get by in Kannada and a little Tamil. One of my coworkers, who lived not far from me and whose son took swim lessons at the same time as my daughter, was from the north of India, and he spoke Marathi and Hindi. At the little Indian grocery and take-out place near my house, I hear Tamil. Some of my neighbors speak Rajasthani.

In my city, the three big languages after English are Spanish, Hmong, and Somali. They are common enough to be semi-official. For example, they appear among notices at the bus stop and some emails from my kids' school.

The official language of Ethiopia, Amharic, is spoken in the many Ethiopian restaurants around town. I saw it advertised for a weekly story time for children at a public library.

Listen to, observe, and strike up conversations with your neighbors, the parents of your kids' friends, the workers and customers at the grocery store. Read the signs, the mail, the fliers at the library. You will learn about your neighbors and create the ties that allow your community to thrive.

2. Who Speaks Them Where?

Who speaks these languages, and where do they speak them? Again, like in ecology, we can make note of the "interactions and adaptations" of languages in the linguasphere. The speakers cover the gamut of identities. One notices, for example, that the age demographic of languages other than English skews old in the US. In other words, you will always encounter more older people who speak them than youngsters—who have "adapted" more to the American, English-centered culture.

Along with learning the dynamic of all the languages in your ecolinguistic sphere, you can look at the "niches," as ecologists say, where those languages are spoken today. Geographically, you can see these places. In certain neighborhoods you are more likely to hear a language spoken, such as Somali in the Cedar-Riverside neighborhood of Minneapolis or Hmong on the East Side of St. Paul. You may find restaurants or shops or even community centers where languages are spoken. Some are more temporary, such as a place of worship where a language is only spoken once a week. They may appear even less often, such as when I discovered a Dakota dialect spoken by a few folks at a local festival near me that only takes place once a year. A whole range of languages are often spoken in individual homes, which is how we measure the level of multilingualism in the US census. Such homes may cluster in particular areas of town.

Among the examples above, I notice different dynamics among the individual speakers, depending on the language community their children participate in and the depth of relationships they have with multiple speakers of the community language. Parents create such linguistic environments to varying degrees. I hear lots of little kids speaking Spanish and Somali in the store, but fewer Hmong children. My Oromo friends speak a mix of Oromo and English to their children. Russians who came to the US when they were about eight or younger as monolingual Russian-speakers grow up speaking their first language with a distinct American accent.

How much children speak the languages comes down to the sacrifice of the parents—and the influence of grandparents and other close loved ones. My friend's children speak wonderful Russian, thanks to the focused homeschool efforts of the mother to pass on her native language. Their Russian grandmother came over once a year to stay for several months, as well. They even put the kids in school for half a year in their mother's hometown in Siberia.

Some friends of ours in Minnesota are a couple from Madrid, and they sent their kids to visit Grandma all summer, every summer, during their childhood. She does not speak a word of English, and the only thing to do in their part of town is walk around the neighborhood and go to the pool with the local kids they hang out with year after year. Even as they finish high school, their Spanish is perfect.

My coworker is married to a Japanese woman. They take their sons to Japanese school every weekend, where they speak Japanese, as well as learn how to read and write. Similarly, they visit their grandmother every summer where they go to school, play soccer, and go on class trips. The boys *love* playing with the other boys there, speaking only in Japanese in their small town.

In my limited observations, I noticed a socio-economic aspect to who speaks what language, and even a relationship to certain jobs. While Spanish is spoken by so many people, I hear it spoken most often in my neighborhood during the summer among roofers and gardeners. Several of my friends testify to learning Spanish by working in restaurant kitchens, as well. I hear Hmong often in farmers markets, where these family farmers talk among themselves as they sell their items. While many Indians work in technology and computers, a Northern Indian friend of mine told me that you find a disproportionate number of Southern Indians, who gravitate towards coding and more technical areas. Sure enough, I hear Tamil and Telugu often among such people at my IT job. I have only heard common European languages, such as French and German, among white-collar workers in the many large corporations in my city. A huge number of Somali-speakers drive taxis and buses. Another sizeable part of the Somali population works as entrepreneurs, starting up small cafes and shops, and these become community meeting places. In some neighborhoods, Somali beats English, spoken by poor and rich, old and young.

Somali cafes with distinct names like *Qoraxlow*, *Tawakal*, and *Deg Deg*, and their friendly, communal customers contributed significantly to how I learned Somali (to the degree that I did). I could go downtown to the Somali Mall, where there were at least three such cafes. After buying a Somali tea (a sweet sort of chai, often with milk), I would sit and watch soccer with the rest of the men. (Women and families often eat in another room.) Either someone would come right up to me and greet me, or I would break the ice with someone next to me. Since I was the elephant in the room, so to speak, as the lone Caucasian, I would tell my neighbor that I was learning Somali and ask if he wanted to help me. He almost always did, and usually more than one other would jump in to help, too, once they overheard our conversation.

My kids' high school put on an amazing Somali Cultural Night, that consisted of drama, dancing, and a fashion show. I will never forget the skit the kids put on, as nearly the entire production was in Somali—much of it improvised—based on their daily experience at school. A Somali mother finds out her son has been hiding his failing grades, so she and her sisters all harangue him to tears. Then, they go to the school to speak with the teachers and principal. Hilarity ensued as the stereotypical Somali mothers and aunties kissed and hugged and held the hand of the reserved Caucasian Minnesotan women principal and teachers, who did not know how to react. Through the comedy of these awkward interactions, the students depicted the tension between family who did not understand the school system, and a school system who could not understand their family.

In learning Oromo, however, I found it difficult to find groups of strangers I could chat with. There are no specifically Oromo restaurants or cafes, only generically Ethiopian ones that always include speakers of at least Oromo and Amharic, and sometimes Somali and

Anyuak. Some cafes around, however, feature almost exclusively Amharic. A cluster of what my friends and I jokingly refer to as "the Amhara Region of St Paul" includes at least three such locations. I learned that Oromos congregate at churches (slightly more than half here are Christians), so I started hanging around an Oromo church on Saturday mornings until I found someone who would commit to teaching me the language. I discovered the Anyuak language listed on the marquee at a church that I drive past in my town. I showed up one day after the Anyuak service and I met some of the speakers of this Ethiopian language.

One does not have to look hard for Spanish. We have Spanish schools, restaurants of many Hispanic countries, and a Spanish-language theater. I regularly pass by a Spanish-language center for *Alcohólicos Anónimos*, and the posters on some local department stores translate their announcements below the English.

Work can even be its own ecolinguistic sphere. I work at an international company, near our global headquarters. In our main office, I know the Romanian speakers and some of the Somali speakers. I organized Spanish and German practice lunches on occasion for native and non-native speakers. We have a couple major offices in Germany and Switzerland, so I get to speak with them on occasion, either on the phone or on the occasions when they come to the home office. I also know my colleagues in Russia and Serbia, so I chat with them once a month to find out what is going on in their countries (generally and specifically to our company) and to practice my languages. I was excited once when I found out a Moroccan works at our Budapest office, and more recently met an Uzbek speaker.

3. How Did the Linguasphere Develop?

Your language occupies an important niche in a vast web of languages. Learning about how it got where it is can uncover deep social undercurrents in your community and even country. This history parallels ecology as it uncovers "the successional development of [ecolinguistic systems]."

First, look at the majority language. It has a history of how it came to dominate your area. This may be recent, like English in Singapore or even North America, or it may be centuries, like Spanish in Spain that originated with Roman soldiers, or Arabic that settled there with the Muslim conquerors after Muhammad's death. Then, you have the language(s) that have occupied that area for centuries. It may be the language of conquered indigenous peoples, like Dakota in the US, Pitjantjatjara in Australia, or Welsh in the UK. Next, you can delve into the viability of the languages. How much does one language dominate over or accommodate another? In some areas, minority languages are gaining ground, like Basque in Spain. Finally, spend some time on the dead languages of your area. Think about what role they used to have, how that role shifted, and how it finally ended. The members of that community speak another language now, and that story is important, as well.

In talking to multilingual people in my hometown and in other cities, I find that language communities interact in surprising ways. I have met immigrants from Asia and Africa to the US who learn Spanish enthusiastically. One high school boy in Seattle from Eritrea understood his mom's Kunama, and he spoke the Tigrinya of his home and Amharic of the media they consumed. He was learning Spanish in addition to English. I met one high school girl in Minneapolis from Somalia who was learning Spanish because her best friend at school was from Mexico. A couple of Palestinian friends of mine from Kuwait ran a grocery store in a heavily Hispanic neighborhood, and they learned it to communicate better with their customers. A couple years ago we hosted a friend from Spain who spoke very little English. When we sent her off into the airport by herself for her return, I told her that if she runs into trouble, talk to a Somali—they usually speak some Spanish.

The languages of East Africa are fluid among their speakers in the US. I was paying at a parking garage after work in St. Paul, and I traded a few pleasantries with the woman in Somali. When I left I said, *"Mahadsanid!"* ("Thank you" in Somali). She responded, *"Galatooma!"*— "thank you" but in Oromo, her language. Whenever I accidentally use a Somali word while speaking Oromo, my friends quickly identify that the word is Somali—and then get a pretty good laugh.

While I have much less first-hand experience among Southeast Asians, I know that many such languages are spoken in the Twin Cities. Many Hmong-speakers live in the area, but since they come mostly from Laos, but also Thailand and Vietnam (I heard that we do not have a large Chinese Hmong/Miao population here), they also speak some of those languages, depending on the level of education they received. When I was talking to one of my elderly neighbors, he was struggling to communicate in English, but I found out he speaks Khmer, from Cambodia. They offer more areas for me to learn about in my community.

Many parents are frightened or sad because the interaction between English and other languages is usually fraught, with other languages pitching a losing battle against this behemoth. One Russian friend refused to speak English to her child before he went to school because she knew that he needed his Russian to be as strong as possible before the floodgates of English were opened in kindergarten. I see many Oromo parents speaking a mix of the two to their kids but wishing they could grow up speaking their parents' language. Another friend came from Egypt with her two daughters when they were little, and as the girls got older, their Arabic disappeared, and they lost the ability to hold conversations with their father back home. A middle school friend of my daughter, whose family comes from Vietnam, was too ashamed to speak a single word of Vietnamese to me when I asked how to say a few specific words, even though her non-English-speaking grandmother lived with them and she heard it spoken every day.

Individual multilingualism displays important facts about languages. For example, German dominates Zurich, Switzerland. Since most residents speak English, monolingual Americans are accommodated. Locals might be less accommodating to Standard German, even though they all know that dialect, too. A distant cousin of mine there preferred to speak English to me rather than the Standard German of their dominant neighbor to the North. Some Swiss even demand that German expats adjust to the local dialect.

I had to make a diplomatic decision quickly as an interpreter once. At a youth conference in Wrocław, Poland, on New Year's Eve of 1995-96, I volunteered to interpret one of the breakout sessions. Sadly for a few of the participants, my Polish was barely functional, and Czech and Slovak, non-existent. At that time, Soviet domination was a recent memory, which included mandatory Russian in school. For the sake of efficiency, I addressed the Slavs in Russian saying, "I hope you don't mind if I speak Russian. I know you don't like it much, but I know you all understand it." All but one shrugged and nodded. They disliked the language; nevertheless, they saw the practicality of what I was saying. Additionally, I am American; if a Russian had made the same request, it may not have met the same equanimity. Similarly, the Catalonians in the group knew I did not know their language, so they also had no problem conversing with me in Spanish (or *Castellano*, as they say). They may have reacted differently if I had been from Madrid. Like in Switzerland, the smaller people want the larger country to recognize their existence and independence.

Through my informal ecolinguistic survey, I plugged into dynamics of my community of which I was previously unaware. Languages overlapped in surprising ways, and Spanish enjoyed some prestige among immigrants of all linguistic backgrounds. While English clearly dominated, not only did it not exist alone without other languages, but speakers of all languages felt its pressure on their children. Many tried to perpetuate their language among their children as they were able.

The Life of an "Ecolinguist" in Action

A friend of mine in Minneapolis is Ethiopian. He works at an Ethiopian restaurant and with customers and staff speaks mostly Amharic, the most widely-known language of Ethiopia and his restaurant, plus some Oromo and English. His mother, the owner, prefers Oromo, her native language. One time, I saw him sitting at a table with a customer speaking a language I could not even recognize—neither Amharic nor Oromo—so I asked him what it was.

"Swahili," he answered. I learned that he grew up in Kenya before coming to the US.

The native-born White American might find it quite a coincidence that he found another speaker of Swahili in this corner of the Upper Midwest US. In fact, many Somali immigrants were born in refugee camps in Kenya, and they speak Swahili better than the Somali language they got from their parents. As a result, Swahili connected two non-Kenyans in that restaurant in Minneapolis.

The ecolinguist notes, "Swahili: a *lingua franca* of the urban northern Mississippi."

I told a native Kenyan friend one time, "I learned your Swahili slang for Somalis." The Somali civil war prompted tens of thousands of refugees to flee south, so Somalis were common in Nairobi. "*Warya.*" She burst out laughing. "How did you know that?" she managed to get out. "*Warya* means 'Hey you!' in Somali," I answered. Kenyans heard this Somali interjection so much that they just used it to name these newcomers.

The ecolinguist notes, "A Somali word became a Swahili slang."

Even small towns in the US can surprise you with a degree of linguistic diversity. My dad grew up in Fremont, Nebraska, and my grandfather used to speak of the Mexicans who filled the meat-packing factory where he retired from. Sioux Falls, South Dakota, hosts the largest Kunama population from Eritrea in the US and an annual festival. Several thousand Somali immigrants live in St. Cloud, Minnesota, and in Lewiston, Maine.

The ecolinguist notes, "Continue Nilo-Saharan research next summer in South Dakota at the Kunama festival."

After studying this phenomenon at home, I returned to Ukraine a couple times and noticed such linguistic complexities in other countries, as well. When I worked in Lviv, in Western Ukraine, my native Russian-speaking friend from Eastern Ukraine, who always spoke Russian in Kyiv, made every effort to speak Ukrainian with strangers.

Everyone understood Russian, but she wanted to show respect. Ten years later, I saw the same phenomenon with another native Russian-speaking colleague.

Note, "Ukrainians speak Ukrainian out of respect for (fear of?) Western Ukrainians."

While this sounds like a scientific pursuit, I was anything but objective. I did not want to study language; I wanted to live in language. The language would live in me as I "lived" the experiment subjectively and not as an objective observer. Learning the language allowed me to become the subject as I connected with new friends, who invited me into their communities. Studying language grew from the root of "loving language," without which I may not have discovered ecolinguism.

PART II
LOVING LANGUAGE

CHAPTER 4
MY STORY OF LANGUAGE LOST

The Ecolinguist of the Future

So excited by learning a handful of Somali, I tried to use it whenever I could. If I overheard it on the bus, if I saw a cashier who looked Somali, if kids were sitting bored in the library lobby, I would toss out a couple words. Often, I would get a surprised look or a smile, but often the words that came back were English.

Thinking out a couple decades, I wondered if these fully bilingual kids would be teaching their children Somali. Looking back a couple decades at the fate of the second language of children and grandchildren in the local Russian émigré community, I saw that Somalis probably would not. Some kids are reluctant to learn it; some even hate their parents' language, whatever it is, and refuse to speak it, not to mention teach it. Languages come to the US to die.

When she was about twelve years old, my daughter invited a friend over for dinner. I found out that her family—parents and grandparents—immigrated from Vietnam. I was excited, so I asked if she spoke Vietnamese.

"No." She avoided looking at my eyes. I had gotten used to this response from middle-schoolers, so I did not pay attention to it.

"Oh, come on. I'm sure you know a little bit."

"No." Still no eye-contact.

I knew that her home included three generations. "How do you talk to your grandmother?"

"She can speak a little English."

"But your parents must talk to her in Vietnamese."

Silence.

"OK. When your mother wants to leave with your grandmother, how does she say, 'Come on, let's go!'?"

"I don't know."

Still no eye-contact. I gave up.

Looking at the number of languages that have arrived in North America, and the number already here when Europeans first showed up on these shores, we see an overall loss of language. Many Americans and Europeans see this as an inevitable result of two unequally matched languages running into each other. In this line of thinking—usually followed by those who have no experience living an entire life in a foreign language—some languages are more dominant, so speakers of less dominant languages simply pivot to the more dominant one. Others claim that certain languages convey "modern" or "technological" thinking better than others, so through a sort of natural selection, one language comes out on top. People turn from their native language to the new one, and their children, seeing the writing on the wall, inevitably adopt the majority language as their own and forget that of their parents. They cast as preordained that the meeting of two languages ends with one dominating the other to extinction.

Yet, I read about the mixed-language communities where multiple languages have interacted together for centuries. One person from the Basque Country in Spain told me that in her town, some people are more comfortable in Basque, others in Spanish, so each speaks the one they want, and everyone understands each other. My friend, a White American, married someone from Malaysia. He remarked that when his wife goes into a shop in her country, she and the shopkeeper subtly, almost unconsciously, negotiate what language they would speak as each throws out a little of different languages to see who is most comfortable in which one. As I studied, I remarked similar situations in Switzerland, India, and Ghana, and even in the ancient Persian and Roman Empires.

What was different in the US compared to these other cultures? As I pursued ecolinguism, the fact of linguistic violence kept rearing its head. Languages do not simply die in the US; they are killed.

Execution of a Family Language

Little Switzerland on the Prairie

My maternal grandmother came from American German stock. While both of her parents were born in the US, her paternal grandparents came from Germany, and her maternal grandparents from German-speaking Switzerland.

When I was in high school, my family traveled to Switzerland to meet "the relatives": my maternal grandmother's cousins' families. My great-grandmother was dedicated to keeping in touch with these relatives and passed these connections down to her children and grandchildren, for which I am grateful. One of my grandmother's cousins remembered Anna, my great-grandmother, who was born in the US, in the small town of Columbus, Nebraska. These Swiss elders told me that she spoke perfectly the dialect of Basel, Switzerland, the birthplace of her parents.

A few decades after this visit, I researched my grandmother's family and discovered some articles written about her maternal grandfather. Samuel Gass was born in Anveil (or Anvil), in Canton Basel, Switzerland, on June 3, 1854. He traveled to Columbus, Nebraska, and spent some time in California. Once settled in Nebraska, he went home to Switzerland, got engaged, and returned. On October 12, 1883, he married his wife, Anna, and his in-laws arrived to live with them. Their daughter—my great-grandmother, Anna—was born on August 8, 1884 and was followed by seven surviving children. Before his death on June 21, 1928, Samuel served several Swiss and German societies, including the Sons of Hermann, in his small town.[6]

Researching this family line afforded me the pleasure to imagine this Swiss-German enclave on the American Prairie, where my great-grandmother spoke her patrimonial Swiss dialect with parents, grand-parents, brothers, sisters, and probably neighbors and other community members. Teachers may have even taught in German. Since German was the second-most widely spoken language in the US at the time, living one's life in it should not surprise us. I knew my great-grandmother, and in spite of this upbringing of hers I never noticed any accent in English. (My mother confirmed this memory.) She was perfectly bilingual.

Language Death

As I researched my family languages further, a fact struck me: my grandmother, the daughter of my great-grandmother Anna, spoke no German other than a couple garbled nursery rhymes. My great-grand-mother spoke the local Swiss dialect perfectly and even married a German American from Missouri. Both surely spoke German all the time, but they did not pass it down.

In this end of a language, I saw another opportunity that my grand-mother had not passed down. My mom, sister, cousins, and uncles and I sometimes dream what would have happened if my grandmother had applied for Swiss citizenship. Had she—or her mother on her behalf—followed this simple process, we all could have had the opportunity to apply for citizenship to Switzerland and all the imagined opportunities that additional passport would have provided.

Language-loss happened right alongside this loss of foreign citizenship, but the story was larger than my grandmother.

My grandmother was born in 1923, right at the end of a great debate about foreign language education. In the 19th century, communities

---

[6] M. Curry, "History of Platte County," accessed December 8, 2019, http://www.usgennet.org/usa/ne/topic/resources/OLLibrary/Platte/pages/bios/hpcn0130.htm.

taught their children in a myriad of languages, such as, Norwegian, Lithuanian, Czech, and Dutch.[7] German-English public schools were established in Ohio in the middle of that century and became widespread throughout the American Midwest. Teachers were hired and brought over from Germany, and German-language textbooks were printed in the US, depicting German-speaking children as young Americans like any other, surrounded by the US Stars and Stripes and singing patriotic songs about the US *in German*.[8] The US functioned as a multilingual country as it welcomed waves of European immigration. People surely bumped into communication problems occasionally, but this diverse society was functioning in multiple languages.

In the 20th century, however, opinions about foreign education—especially when carried out in German—changed significantly. In the wake of World War I and a century of monumental immigration, nativism created a backlash against foreign-language schools. Presidents Theodore Roosevelt and Woodrow Wilson spoke out explicitly in favor of "unhyphenated Americanism," which believed that Americans must simply be Americans and not Irish-Americans, German-Americans, etc.[9] President Wilson famously said, "[A]ny man who carries a hyphen about with him carries a dagger that he is ready to plunge into the vitals of this Republic whenever he gets ready."[10] He depicted immigrants and their children with allegiance to any other ethnicity as dangerous to the survival of the country.

---

[7] Marguerite Malakoff and Kenji Hakuta, "History of Language Minority Education in the United States," nd, https://web.stanford.edu/~hakuta/www/research/publications/(1990)%20-%20HISTORY%20OF%20LANGUAGE%20MINORITY%20EDUCATION%20IN%20THE%20UNTIE.pdf.

[8] "German-Language Education in America | Max Kade Institute," accessed September 17, 2019, https://mki.wisc.edu/research/culture_traditions/german-language-education-america.

[9] John Higham, *Strangers in the Land: Patterns of American Nativism, 1860-1925* (Rutgers University Press, 2002), 198.

[10] "American Rhetoric: Woodrow Wilson—'Final Address in Support of the League of Nations,'" accessed September 22, 2019, https://www.americanrhetoric.com/speeches/wilsonleagueofnations.htm.

When the US government translated these feelings into legislative action, the German language lay in their crosshairs, though others suffered casualties, as well. Local communities translated this movement into different codes: associations' charters must be in English, no German spoken in the city limits, and the German language forbidden even in some churches. The federal and state governments aimed at the schools, and in October 1918 a bill was advanced to create a Department of Education to restrict funds if states allowed instruction in languages other than English.[11]

In 1919, the year my great-grandmother turned 35 years old and bore her first child (that is, my great-aunt), the State of Nebraska enacted the "Siman Act." It stated, "No person, individually or as a teacher, shall, in any private, denominational, parochial or public school, teach any subject to any person in any language other than the English language."[12] Even learning a foreign language in school was prohibited until after eighth grade. This turned 180 degrees from the previous Mockett Law from six years previous (just before World War I), which required schools to offer foreign-language classes if at least 50 students demanded them.[13] While the Siman Act did not call out any particular language, German was one of the most commonly-spoken languages in the schools after English, and Nebraska was filled with German-speaking immigrants and US-born—like my great-great-grandfather and great-grandmother. Whomever the law was aimed at, it struck the enormous target of the German language.

This conflict came to a head when Robert T. Meyer was an instructor in Zion Lutheran School, a one-room schoolhouse in Hampton, Nebraska. On May 25, 1920, he was teaching the subject of reading in the German language to 10-year-old Raymond Parpart, a fourth

[11] "*Meyer v. Nebraska*," in *Wikipedia*, September 8, 2019, https://en.wikipedia.org/w/index.php?title=Meyer_v._Nebraska&oldid=914557662.

[12] "*Meyer v. Nebraska*."

[13] Jim McKee, "Jim McKee: Nebraska School Case Ended up in the U.S. Supreme Court," JournalStar.com, April 3, 2011, https://journalstar.com/news/local/jim-mckee-nebraska-school-case-ended-up-in-the-u/article_feb4df8c-7f0c-5ad9-931c-38508baf3858.html.

grader. Frank Edgerton, the County Attorney of Hamilton County, Nebraska, visiting the school on that day, overheard the lesson and charged Meyer with violating the Siman Act.[14]

The fine of $25 was challenged and made its way to the Nebraska State Supreme Court, where the decision was upheld citing the "baneful effects of permitting foreigners . . . to rear and educate their children in the language of their native land," with results "inimical to our own safety."[15] *Safety.* Foreign language education is dangerous, they claimed. Anti-German sentiment, expressed in linguistic sanctions, permeated the Nebraska legislation and jurisprudence, which reflected overwhelmingly vocal popular sentiment.[16]

Nevertheless, the Siman Act was overturned three years later by the US Supreme Court in the famous 1923 decision, *Meyer v. Nebraska,* where the Court held that restricting foreign-language education violated the Due Process clause of the Fourteenth Amendment.[17]

In spite of the ultimate vindication of using languages other than English in education, the period of World War I struck a fatal blow to multilingualism in Nebraska and the rest of the country. Justice McReynolds said in the *Meyer* decision, "Mere knowledge of the German language cannot reasonably be regarded as harmful. Heretofore

---

[14] McKee.

[15] Christopher Capozzola, *Uncle Sam Wants You: World War I and the Making of the Modern American Citizen* (Oxford University Press, 2008), 194.

[16] "War Hysteria & the Persecution of German-Americans," accessed September 17, 2019, https://www.historyonthenet.com/authentichistory/1914-1920/2-homefront/4-hysteria/. In Minnesota, my current state of residence, the Minnesota Commission of Public Safety (MCPS) was created by the state legislature in April of 1917 and headed by Governor J. A. A. Burnquist. Its wide-reaching authority purported to support the domestic front and confront disloyalty. Among other activities, the commission kept a close watch on German Americans, who were also considered suspicious because of their espousing socialism and pacifism. (See "Anti-German Nativism, 1917–1919 | MNopedia," accessed September 17, 2019, http://www.mnopedia.org/anti-german-nativism-1917-1919.) Hence, the actions and popular views in Nebraska were not limited to that state.

[17] "*Meyer v. Nebraska.*"

it has been commonly looked upon as helpful and desirable."[18] Within the justice's memory and current understanding, knowing multiple languages was considered beneficial. *Heretofore*, but no longer.

The social effects permanently changed my family, as society continued to change in an anti-German direction. Significantly, Meyer's crime was committed sixty miles away and one year after the birth of my grandmother's older sister. I do not know what my great-grandmother's family knew of the Siman Act or of *Meyer v. Nebraska*. The atmosphere for German Americans could not have been good outside the German enclaves of Columbus, with political power in the hands of zealous attorneys general looking to fine teachers for germinating the seeds of the destruction of the nation. A few years after my great-great-grandfather led his local chapter of the Sons of Hermann, the chapter in New Ulm, Minnesota, 300 miles away from him, disbanded and donated their famous public sculpture to the city in 1929.[19] My great-grandmother did not apply for Swiss citizenship for her children. Comprehensive German education ended. Struck a fatal blow in the language, German and Swiss culture in the US were dying—killed.

The Siman Act arose as part of a multi-pronged attack against Germans and "foreignness," and the *Meyer* victory could not turn society back. World War I introduced hordes of anti-German propaganda dehumanizing them by depicting them as brutes.[20] Not only speaking German but being German were declared "inimical" to safety by the Nebraska Supreme Court, leaving these people vulnerable in this period.

[18] *"Meyer v. Nebraska."*
[19] "Sons of Hermann," in *Wikipedia*, July 8, 2019, https://en.wikipedia.org /w/index.php?title=Sons_of_Hermann&oldid=905366685.
[20] "Germany–United States Relations," in *Wikipedia*, October 14, 2021, https://en.wikipedia.org/w/index.php?title=Germany%E2%80%93United_States_ relations&oldid=1049846329.

Multilingualism as Mortal Enemy

While this situation was well-publicized, we can witness unrecognized downstream effects of this linguistic nativism in education. Many native Nebraskans were speaking Czech and Russian and other languages during the late 19th century. In my childhood in the 1980s, nevertheless, I did not hear Czech at the Czech festival of Wilbur, Nebraska. A couple years ago, my Danish friend noted that he did not hear more than a few words of Danish at the Danish festival in Elkhorn, Iowa. As a teen I did not hear Dutch at the Dutch festival in Denver.

The belief that languages other than English could destroy America as we knew it implies that the US must be an exclusively English-speaking country so that we might preserve our safety. Unlike in most other countries, US officials depicted multilingualism as an existential threat. As a result of this stance, destroying other languages meant defeating potential enemies.

As we see the effects on my White family, this sentiment came down harder on Black individuals and Native peoples. The languages that Black people had brought with them from Africa had long-ago been annihilated. As we will see in the next chapter, a raft of policies over the course of the 19th and 20th centuries ensured the weakening and attempted extermination of indigenous languages; whole languages would become extinct. The story of my European family only represented the tip of the iceberg of linguistic violence.

One time the mother of my daughter's Vietnamese friend came to drop her off. As she was leaving, her van got stuck in our snowy street, so I came out to help. After success in freeing it up, we began to chat. I asked her name, and she gave me her "American" name. I asked for her name in Vietnamese, and she said it. After I practiced pronouncing it a few times, she gave me the thumbs-up and drove away.

The next time I saw her daughter, I mentioned her mother by name. She looked right at me that time, but struggled against me, first denying it was her name. Then she told me I was saying it wrong, even when I reminded her that her mother confirmed I pronounced it correctly.

My grandmother was christened "Emma," but went by "Jo" as long as I knew her. She told me that she unofficially changed it after associating it with "Emma the Fat Lady" at a circus side-show—but now I wondered. Perhaps it sounded too "German" to her Americanized ears, conditioned to love English only. American society looked harshly on Germans at this time, and many "Schmidts" were becoming "Smiths" and "Müllers," "Millers." Hence, she grabbed onto a much more English and stylish (for the 1930s) name.

When I think back on the dinner with my daughter's friend, I wonder what my great-grandmother thought when "Swiss-American" was a mortal enemy of the United States and when a German teacher was fined for teaching in the same language Anna spoke with her parents and grandparents. It no longer surprises me when I see the children of Somali immigrants struggle to speak the language of their parents. We have allowed our country to be defined by the *exclusive* use of the English language, and these American East African kids—in addition to my American Swiss grandmother and my American Vietnamese daughter's friend—want to be just American, even at the expense of losing their linguistic birthright.

To this day, speaking a foreign language bears two seemingly contradictory connotations. A native English-speaker who learns three foreign languages: helpful and desirable. An immigrant to the US bringing three languages to their first English class: subversive. Even speaking English with an accent can elicit the heated reaction, "Why don't you speak English?" Our society sends an overwhelming message: bilingualism endangers our country more than ignorant monolingualism.

CHAPTER 5

PAST LINGUISTIC VIOLENCE

The permanent loss of languages and ways of life sadden me with a humanity impoverished. I watched the 2010 documentary, "Voices in the Clouds," about a Taiwanese-American man, Tony Coolidge, who reconnected to his Atayal (one of the indigenous peoples of Taiwan) heritage after the death of his mother. Coolidge linked up with activists who were working to preserve the heritage of the various indigenous cultures of this Island.

I had mixed reactions to this film. On the one hand, the Atayal children amazed me as they sang and danced with such passion and skill beyond their years. Their teacher's success is known internationally. The film also highlighted those who continued traditional handicrafts, especially beautiful embroidery.

On the other hand, the movie conspicuously lacked people speaking the Atayal language. Most of the movie was in English and Mandarin. I am assuming the songs were in the native languages. I did not, however, hear any Atayal conversations. When Coolidge met one of the Atayal elders and introduced himself, the woman immediately asked in Mandarin, "Do you speak Atayal?" The answer was "no," so the conversation continued in Mandarin. My heart sank, as the woman's perhaps did, as well.

To me, a loss was palpable without the language; it felt like looking at a museum. Rather than depicting the Atayal living and communicating in their most normal way, which happened to be Atayal, the life and crafts and music were about preservation. Even though the Atayal speak their language regularly with each other,[21] the film gave the

---

[21] "Many Atayal are bilingual, but the Atayal language still remains in active use. ("Atayal People," in *Wikipedia*, January 22, 2021, https://en.wikipedia.org/

impression of "living history"–but history all the same. One very old woman talked about life in her mountain village, before she moved to the city: "We used to sing in the trees." They simply sang; they did not sing to preserve a culture.[22]

A living language communicates all things. With it, you bargain at the market, you flirt with someone, you ask questions from your teacher, you listen to your grandparents' and your children's stories, you sing beloved songs with your friends—and write new ones. Once these areas are closed off to your language, your language begins to die.

While we find records of this language-loss in Taiwan only with difficulty, we can see how the process unfolded in the United States. In my country, policies motivated by "helping" Native Americans by annihilating their languages succeeded in dehumanizing the original inhabitants of this land through physical and emotional violence.

Killing Bilingual(i)s(m)

We all know that the indigenous languages of the Americas began to decline upon the arrival of Europeans to the New World. As whole peoples were starved, died of disease, and were otherwise killed, their languages accompanied them to the grave. While some peoples survived, their languages have died or find themselves mortally imperiled

---

w/index.php?title=Atayal_people&oldid=1002105584.)

[22] The history of the aboriginal peoples of Taiwan is relatively obscure. One reads often of the traders from Europe and China asserting and reasserting control of the island from the 16th century to today. Native history, however, is muddled. Therefore, I have not found a complete history describing the disappearance of local culture. One can read hints of imperial policy that could have contributed to the loss of native culture and language in one article that says, "Wild barbarians were the most heavily taxed, civilized barbarians less so, and the Han Chinese the least of all. Naturally, civilized barbarians were eager to become Han Chinese. During the Qing era, aborigines who expressed a desire to become Chinese were given names like Lin or Wang" (Kenryo Lin, "The Taiwanese are not Han Chinese," *Society for the Dissemination of Historical Fact* [blog], accessed October 10, 2019, http://www.sdh-fact.com/essay-article/418/).

today. The domination of the English language, and before that, Spanish, led to the extinction of uncounted indigenous tongues.

While some believe that the Native American languages simply "disappeared" among the surviving peoples because English somehow passively "took over," that it was an inevitable result of English being a superior or more viable language, the number of dead languages uprooted by our colonial plow was deliberate and avoidable. Plenty of societies show a mix of languages. In the example of Basque in Spain, it continued on and is growing today, after its speakers were conquered by Romans, Arabs, and the Spanish.

The US created special conditions to kill indigenous languages more efficiently than its neighbors. Mexico in 2005 included almost 7% of the population who spoke indigenous languages.[23] In Canada, recent numbers show that 0.6% of the population speaks an indigenous language.[24] While this percentage is very small, it towers over the 0.1% of the US population who speaks a Native American language.[25] Empirically, therefore, the "disappearance" of indigenous languages in the US was more thorough than in other societies, which puts doubt on the "inevitability" of language death and raises the question of the conditions unique to the US.

As the United States expanded as a country, documents show that the value of Native American languages was, in fact, debated among

---

[23] "Mexico–Languages," Statista, accessed October 4, 2019, https://www.statista.com/statistics/275440/languages-in-mexico/.

[24] Statistics Canada Government of Canada, "Proportion of Mother Tongue Responses for Various Regions in Canada, 2016 Census," August 4, 2017, https://www12.statcan.gc.ca/census-recensement/2016/dp-pd/dv-vd/lang/index-eng.cfm.

[25] The 2010 census counted 6.1 million American Indians and Alaskan Natives, and 364,776 speak Navajo or other Native American language. Since the total population of the country was 291,524,091 at that time, the percent of Native American language speakers is just over 0.1% in the US (U. S. Census Bureau, "American FactFinder-Results," accessed October 4, 2019, https://factfinder.census.gov/faces/tableserices/jsf/pages/productview.xhtml?eml=gd&pid=PEP_2015_PEPASR5H&prodType=table&utm_medium=email&utm_source=govdelivery; Camille Ryan, "Language Use in the United States: 2011," American Community Survey Reports, August 2013, 1–16).

those of European ancestry. William Penn, the founder of Philadelphia in the colony of Pennsylvania that bears his name, for example, esteemed learning the language of the neighboring Lenape so that he could negotiate with them directly. In his view at that time, he explained, "I have made it my business to understand [the Lenape language], that I might not want an Interpreter on any occasion...."[26]

Officials did not immediately advocate the imposition of English; in Penn's day, English may not have even been the majority language among European settlers. The eventual extreme violence that underlay the US program of "forgetting" indigenous languages formed the unique conditions here. These languages did not "die" or "perish," as we often read; they were murdered ruthlessly based on the philosophical and political ideals that won the day. US policy evolved from Penn's coexistence, and then the benign growth of literacy, and finally the imposition of violence.

Literacy

When Europeans initially encountered the estimated 300 languages of North America, they worked to communicate in a multilingual fashion.[27] In 1660 John Eliot published the first Bible in British North America in the Natick dialect of the Massachusett language. While sent as a missionary to convert the natives of the New World, he decided that he would advance his cause more effectively by learning the local language rather than trying to teach them English. He followed in a centuries-old tradition of missionaries who created a written language from scratch. Then he translated the Bible into their language. With a written Natick Bible, he only needed to teach the natives to read their own language.[28]

---

[26] William Penn, *William Penn's Own Account of the Lenni Lenape Or Delaware Indians*, ed. Albert Cook Myers (B B& A Publishers, 1970), 22.

[27] "Indigenous Languages of the Americas," in *Wikipedia*, August 31, 2019, https://en.wikipedia.org/w/index.php?title=Indigenous_languages_of_the_Americas&oldid=913280279.

[28] "*Eliot Indian Bible*," in *Wikipedia*, September 29, 2019, https://en.wikipedia.org/w/index.php?title=Eliot_Indian_Bible&oldid=918571794.

Educating Native Americans focused on literacy for the next several hundred years, which the US began funding in 1819. By the early 19th century, textbooks had been written in the Chippewa (also known as Ojibwe) and some Siouan languages. Educators reported in 1871 how quickly and eagerly natives acquired literacy in their own languages. One missionary teacher at this time reported that three Yankton Sioux warriors traveled 40 miles weekly on horseback to acquire the tools to read and write.[29] Local teachers found native-language education successful for educating their students.

At the same time, teachers struggled to pass on fluency in English. Reporting on one disappointed educator in Nebraska, a member of a missionary board wrote,

> She went on for a year teaching these [Native American] scholars, which the agent, her especial friend, secured, almost compelling them to attend, and at the end of the year these scholars could read English beautifully, could spell English beautifully, and could write English beautifully, and they did not understand the first word of English.[30]

Students could master the skill of reading and writing but this report illustrates that they did not internalize English.

The fact that they were so good regarding the *skills* of English, makes me wonder if the students were actually completely ignorant of the "first word of English." This may have hyperbolically expressed the teacher's frustration at making the students English-speakers. It resonates too closely with what I heard from monolingual anglophones at work who complained that the call center help desk agents in the Philippines "can't speak English," when they are in fact describing a non-native English speaker who speaks it a bit slower or with an accent. Surely, the Native American students communicated with their teacher, even if through a strong foreign accent. Perfect bilingualism—that is, flawless, native speakers of English—did not result in

---

[29] Jon Reyhner, "American Indian Language Policy and School Success," accessed September 29, 2019, http://jan.ucc.nau.edu/~jar/BOISE.html.

[30] Jon Reyhner.

these classrooms, but their level of ignorance could likely have been misunderstood or exaggerated by English monolingual educators.

Displaying a shift from Penn's and Eliot's stances, the teachers of the Dakota clearly did not know the local languages. A local Dakota newspaper editorial in 1874 mocked these teachers attempting to force English on students, writing,

> It is sheer laziness in the teacher to berate his Indian [sic] scholars for not understanding English, when he does not understand enough Indian [sic] to tell them the meaning of a single one of the sentences he is trying to make them understand properly, though they have no idea of the sense. The teacher with his superior mind, should be able to learn half a dozen languages while these children of darkness are learning one. Even though the teacher's object were only to have them master English, he had better teach it to them in Indian [sic], so they may understand what they are learning.[31]

While clear, ugly prejudices against Native American intellect are imbedded—or, perhaps, lampooned—in this statement, the belief holds true that teachers who teach a foreign language should themselves be capable of learning at least one, if not a "half a dozen." If these teachers believe themselves to be so intellectually superior to their students, their monolingual ignorance of the Dakota ("Indian") language does not reflect the multilingual aspirations for their students. The students' weaknesses in actually learning English overshadowed their teachers' complete unwillingness to acquire another language. Perfect Dakota plus mediocre English totaled less than perfect English alone. Already we see that a monolingual English speaker was worth more than a multilingual who learned English later.

---

[31] Jon Reyhner. Clearly, calling the language "Indian" obscures the variety of Native American languages. I have kept it, nevertheless, in quotations from contemporary sources, where it appears to refer to the Dakota language.

Forced to Forget

Educational philosophy shifted from bilingualism towards nativist monolingualism. Some teachers attempted to teach English in the native language of the students. An ideological struggle ensued, however, that pitted those educators who supported first-language education against those nativist federal officials, who wanted English only, who wanted bilingualism slashed to monolingualism. In 1880 the Indian Bureau followed the latter line and declared that all instruction must be in English—even forbidding textbooks printed in native languages—under the threat of cutting off school funding.

A few years later, policy was ratcheted up and declared, "All instruction shall be in the English language. Pupils shall be required to converse with employees and each other in English. All school employees must be able to speak English fluently."[32] Teaching philosophy thus went beyond forcing children to learn English to forbidding any language other than English in the school. Students could not even speak their language to each other at school. Speaking English "fluently" could very well have been used to exclude non-native English speakers. An 1887 official report expressed the philosophical underpinnings of this policy.

> Nothing so surely and perfectly stamps upon an individual a national characteristic as language.... [As the Native Americans] are in an English-speaking country, they must be taught the language which they must use in transacting business with the people of this country. No unity or community of feeling can be established among different peoples unless they are brought to speak the same language, and thus become imbued with like ideas of duty....
>
> The instruction of the Indians [sic] in the vernacular is not only of no use to them, but is detrimental to the cause of their education and civilization, and no school will be

---

[32] Jon Reyhner.

permitted on the reservation in which the English language is not exclusively taught.[33]

The first paragraph does not recognize what people do automatically. Human brains learn the languages they need; you do not need a policy that forces them to do so. If they need to conduct business, people learn the necessary language. When I lived in Morocco, I saw children of 12 years old able to do business in the market with tourists in a half-dozen languages—and they maybe learned one in school, if they attended.

This report expressed superiority and chauvinism under the pleasant mask of "unity." The ideology bears a double thrust. First, speaking a single language in common is a prerequisite to "community of feeling." In other words, a single society requires that all members speak the same language to instill the same notions of duties and communal feelings. Moreover, the report asserts that they must conduct business in English, which showed how this policy foreshadows the anti-German policy I described previously, and the phrase "English-speaking country" silences whole education systems in other European languages at that time. Second, speaking Native American languages harms the speakers themselves. The writer confused correlation with causation. The Native Americans appeared "uncivilized" and "uneducated" and they spoke another language, so the twisted reasoning concluded that their language caused—at least in part—their so-called inferiority. Civilization and education, furthermore, can only exist apart from such languages.

While my examples of Spain, Malaysia, and Switzerland showed that the first point is empirically false, the second point is both less provable and more dangerous. Technically, the first point allows bilingualism, as long as one of the languages is a single, national one. Bahasa Malaysia functions this way. Significantly, Switzerland does not have a single national language, yet it is difficult to say that they lack "community of feeling." The second point eliminates the possibility of bilingualism because the "other" language is inherently bad and

---

[33] Jon Reyhner.

destructive. The latter point, therefore, lays the groundwork for the ensuing racist scorched-earth campaign against all languages.

Some educators of the time taught English, but nevertheless, pushed back against English-only. Some fought for first-language education based on the evidence of the time, albeit anecdotal. Namely, education that banished native languages was not effective in its pedagogical goal.

> Our missionaries feel very decidedly on this point, and that is as to their work in the teaching of English. They believe that it can be better done by using Dakota also, and that it will be done by them in their regular educational methods. While it is not true that we teach only English, it is true that by beginning in the Indian tongue [sic] and then putting the students into English studies our missionaries say that after three or four years their English is better than it would have been if they had begun entirely with English.[34]

Experience already showed in 1880 that English-only education delayed acquisition of English. (Educators are still arguing this point to the present day.) The educators argued that teaching students in Dakota and respecting the fact of their language *supported* the goal of teaching them English. Therefore, the government's ideology about excluding other languages *undermined* the prerequisite for common discourse in English.

The government, unfortunately, dug in its heels on its strong English-only position, and boarding schools began to dominate.[35] In local schools, students learned English in the classroom and spoke native languages at home. The residential system coerced—sometimes by force—children to relocate away from their families, and thereby

---

[34] Jon Reyhner.

[35] While any expression of native culture was forbidden in those institutions, for example, boys growing long hair, I will focus here on the linguistic aspect of control. ("American Indian Boarding Schools," in *Wikipedia*, September 15, 2019, https://en.wikipedia.org/w/index.php?title=American_Indian_boarding_schools&oldid=915834816.)

successfully compelled the use of English alone. Punishments for linguistic transgressions were brutal: washing students' mouths out with lye soap for speaking their languages, and worse. One scholar wrote,

> The foremost requirement for assimilation into American society, authorities felt, was mastery of the English language. Commissioner of Indian Affairs T.J. Morgan described English as *"the language of the greatest, most powerful and enterprising nationalities beneath the sun."* Such chauvinism did not allow for bilingualism in the boarding schools. Students were prohibited from speaking their native languages and those caught "speaking Indian" were severely punished. Later, many former students regretted that they lost the ability to speak their native language fluently because of the years they spent in boarding school.[36]

The cruelty was so effective that students faced language and cultural barriers when they returned to their homes unable to converse with parents and relatives.[37] Through violence and humiliation, American education laid an axe to the root of connection between students and their forefathers.

It is easy to underestimate the active decision to destroy languages other than English, killing them rather than letting them die. The US government was waging an ideological, social war. "Mastery of English" was foremost rhetorically but undermined in policy and in fact. They seemed rhetorically to agree with the reservation educators, that learning English was important, but the latter had a better way for students to master English by beginning with first-language education. Foremost for federal policymakers was, in fact, not students' "mastering" English, but English "mastering" the students, to the point of *extinction* of native languages. Focusing on students' mastery of English

---

[36] Carolyn J. Marr, "Assimilation Through Education: Indian Boarding Schools in the Pacific Northwest," accessed October 4, 2019, https://content.lib.washington.edu/aipnw/marr.html.

[37] "American Indian Boarding Schools."

actually allows bilingualism; mastery of English over native languages does not. The choice of the phrase "lost the ability to speak" sadly silences the inhuman suffering the schools employed to vivisect these societies linguistically.

A shift in educational focus took place in the last quarter of the 19th century. The previous focus on general literacy moved to one on English literacy. From there, political ideologues decided that they could achieve English-language hegemony only through the extinction of other languages, that the continued existence of native language-speakers threatened the United States. This narrow notion of US security thus necessitated monolingualism.

The Battle Continues

The rare use of Native American languages spoken in school today can still provoke harsh reactions. In 2012, Miranda Washinawatok, a Menominee girl in Wisconsin, was punished when the 12-year-old pronounced three words of her native language. Julie Gurta, her teacher, angrily responded, "You are not to speak like that. How do I know you're not saying something bad? How would you like it if I spoke in Polish and you didn't understand?" Bilingualism still threatens our security.

In a later statement, Ms. Gurta stated, "Language and behavior that creates a possibility of elitism, or simply excludes other students, can create or increase racial and cultural tensions."[38] Ironically, Ms. Gurta reinforced the elitism—mastery—of English in the classroom, perhaps thinking that speaking English was somehow more neutral or equal. "Exclusion" for her meant excluding English-only speakers, not excluding Menominee-speakers. The exclusive use of English in Wisconsin came at the cost of ideological and physically violent

---

[38] Laura Hibbard, "Miranda Washinawatok, Wisconsin Student Punished for Using Native Tongue, Receives Apology from School, Diocese," HuffPost, March 2, 2012, https://www.huffpost.com/entry/miranda-washinawatok-student-receives-apology-from-school-_n_1316407. See also Richard Benton, "Definitely *not* Loving Language," *Loving Language* (blog), March 3, 2012, https://loving-language.wordpress.com/2012/03/03/definitely-not-loving-language/.

elitism for over one hundred years—the very elitism Ms. Gurta apparently repudiated.

True linguistic egalitarianism would mean everyone learn the languages of their classmates, for example, Ms. Gurta learn Menominee and Ms. Washinawatok, Polish. (For the sake of equity, though, maybe Ms. Gurta should learn first.) Desiring inclusion in the classroom, and knowing the history of the interaction between the two languages, Menominee and English (plus Polish), would lead one to establish them both as viable languages in the classroom.

This philosophical move from viable multilingualism to ideological monolingualism not only shredded indigenous societies, but also tore the soul of the entire US. After the violent actions arising from this decision, the US continued to double down on monolingualism. Our treatment of our First Nations determined how we would continue to view and act towards other languages besides English.

CHAPTER 6
PRESENT LINGUISTIC VIOLENCE

Linguistic violence continues, but it has added subtle and sophisticated forms that do not require kidnapping and washing kids' mouths out with soap at school. When we do not make a space for them, languages—along with their speakers—are themselves vulnerable to the existential violence that leads to their demise. While violence may only target individuals, the community as a whole is subject to death by a thousand cuts. Languages do not die of neglect; they are killed. This violence follows three themes:

1. *Physical.* An act of physical violence to prevent speaking a language, from corporal punishment in schools or punching someone in the face, to genocide. Threats of bodily harm make speaking a language result in pain, which forever connects the language with that wound. At the extreme, killing the speakers of a language obliterates the memory of that language from humanity.

2. *Economic.* An act that cuts off speakers of a language from supporting themselves, impoverishing the language community as a whole. For example, English-only workplaces restrict or cut off workers' ability to use their native language by threatening to fire them. Businesses can also restrict or forbid customers from speaking certain languages.

3. *Social.* An act that deploys shame against language-speakers. Shame includes, for example, non-physical violence towards school children in either active mockery or in subtler forms of condescension, such as the Menominee example in the previous chapter. Peer pressure can also play a part.

I set these in order of visibility because linguistic violence can be happening when English-speakers do not realize it. These acts and the systems that encourage them operate "under the radar"—whether in boarding schools or break rooms—where they are difficult to detect for some, at times even for those to whom they are aimed. Like removing wildflowers and wildlife from our massive corn fields, the battle for monolingualism requires poison that ultimately sickens the ones who consume its fruits.

The Illogic of Monolingual Communities

Let's think ecolinguistically. Twenty percent of Americans speak another language at home, so we are likely bumping into multilingual people on a fairly regular basis. This seems more intuitive in large urban areas like New York City or Los Angeles, but when I hear about Spanish in Nampa, Idaho, and Hmong in Oshkosh, Wisconsin, I know that an enormous number of native English-speakers has heard at least some other language in their community. Hence, a great number of towns are multilingual, if only to a small degree.

If there is a percentage of people who speak these languages in my community, I would expect some proportion of street signs or public announcements in these languages. I do not see them represented much in such official communications, however. Moreover, I do not overhear as many conversations in public places as I would expect. Let's consider Hmong. Based on my experience, Hmong conversations usually happen because one Hmong-speaker seems more likely to go out with another from the same community. If one in 50 members of my community (2%) speaks Hmong, then I would expect roughly one of every 50 groups of shoppers at the grocery store, one of every 50 gatherings at a restaurant, one of every 50 families at the mall, to speak Hmong. I do not hear Hmong at that proportion in public places. Once you add on the other languages of my community (e.g., Spanish, Somali, Oromo, Russian, Arabic), I would think that I might hear other languages in up to one in ten conversations. While I have not measured, I do not feel that the number is that high.

Some locations produce more abundant numbers of conversations in different languages. At the library, for example, I would expect to hear a good-sized amount, but fewer than in the high school hallways during passing period. My kids would likely hear Hmong every day, or at least a few times per week, in addition to the other languages. Naturally, I would expect my kids—any of the kids in the school community—to grow up with these languages. Stretching a bit, I would imagine Hmong to make up an equivalent percent of their vocabulary, more or less depending on their social circles.

Nevertheless, Hmong does not pop up as often as one might hope.

While people joke about American monolingualism, this state came about from sheer brutality and requires energy to be maintained. It is as difficult to give up our "mother tongue" as it is to give up our mother. We learn from our mother the nature of the mother-child relationship through her words, her songs, her poems, her actions, her attitudes, which she learned from her mother. They are all linked together. The most natural thing in the world is to raise our children in the manner that was imprinted on us since before we were born. Preventing this transmission, therefore, requires extraordinary deprivation and terror; we have to turn people against their own instincts.

At the same time, Americans are known throughout the world not just as speakers of a single language, but also as some of the worst language-learners. In other words, not only do we not speak the languages around us, we cannot learn them even when given the right conditions. We go beyond exterminating our languages: we smothered our own ability to learn them. Children naturally learn multiple languages, so somehow, our society prevents them from doing so.

The analogy to ecology helps us again: we have created an English monocrop like the corn and soybean monocrops we see in the American Midwest. A modern cornfield ideally contains only the species of corn planted plus any animals or microbes that aid the corn's success. Naturally, though, other plants grow, which we call "weeds," as well as other animals, "pests." Through a huge amount of energy, we wage war against these weeds and pests to preserve the single crop of corn as far as the eye can see. This violence against nature poisons water, air, and earth, and depletes the soil so that the coming generations provide less healthful, nutritious food. The soil requires humans to use more energy and chemicals so that corn can continue to grow at all. Eventually, the soil is so depleted that wildflowers could no longer grow on their own if you planted them.

Alternatively, in some Native American cultures in North America, corn is never grown alone, but in a traditional system called the "three sisters." Corn is grown along with beans and squash in a single mound. The beans use the corn stalk to climb up in order to get the sunlight they need while providing nitrates to the soil so the corn and squash can grow stronger and the soil can remain productive. The ground cover of the squash prevents weeds from growing and thus focuses the soil to provide nutrition to the other two. All three crops grow strong without additional chemicals and with less energy that deplete the soil—and can continue to do so for generations. More importantly, the food provides more nutrition per calorie than the mono-crop method.

Cultivating the languages of our ecolinguistic sphere allows them to grow naturally and to complement each other, enriching all of them and their speakers. We want kids to follow nature's lead and to nourish their natural ability to learn languages. As we do so, languages—multiple languages at a time—flourish. We just need to make space for them. My children could be walking down multilingual hallways hearing, and even understanding, languages from every continent. Instead, they might catch a couple non-English words—usually in Spanish or Somali in their school—uttered far beneath the din of a single dominating language. The families of those children may avoid the restaurants and public places I listed above precisely because Americans do not welcome their language. Eliminating languages requires the constant energy of monocropping and leaves our environment just as poisoned and depleted; hence, my children grow up fighting and struggling to learn Spanish in class, rather than by simply hanging out with their native-speaking Spanish classmates and doing what human brains do naturally.

Physical Violence: Hating Swahili

In 2015, a woman physically attacked another woman, leaving her with 15 stitches in her face, for speaking the wrong language.[39] A Somali woman, Asma Jama, was speaking Swahili publicly, in a restaurant with her family in Coon Rapids (a little north of Minneapolis), Minnesota. Hearing this non-English language upset a White, English-monolingual woman, Jodie Marie Burchard-Risch, so she yelled at Jama and then assaulted the Swahili-speaker by dumping a beer on her and smashing her face with the glass.[40]

Cultivating languages still matters for life and death, even in the 21st century. Advocating for a multilingual public space may seem abstract or a "nice-to-have" feature for an ideal society, but physical violence is still a symptom of the sickness brought on by the poison of militant monolingualism.

A large number of Americans feel real fear and anger when they hear a language besides English. They say they fear someone is talking about them, even though they do not march to the back of the restaurant and into the kitchen to smash all the faces of all the English-speakers who may be talking about them, too. Like the Wisconsin teacher, above, they hate the distance and difference between people. They feel isolated and cut off. They sense their inability to understand a foreign language.

Aggression around language-use occurs too often, though usually short of a broken glass. While Jama never experienced it during her first 15 years in the US, I have met plenty of people who suffered heated exchanges because of the language they spoke. One Hispanic student of mine recounted that a White man approached him in a bar

---

[39] I discussed this event elsewhere. See Richard Benton, "Hating Swahili: The Cost of Bilingualism in the US," *Loving Language* (blog), November 12, 2015, https://lovinglanguage.wordpress.com/2015/11/12/hating-swahili-the-cost-of-bilingualism-in-the-us/.

[40] The story takes an interesting turn, wherein the victim and the attacker's sister become friends. (See "Dawn Sahr and Asma Jama," accessed December 8, 2019, https://storycorps.org/stories/dawn-sahr-and-asma-jama-170721/.)

and aggressively asked him about speaking Spanish, "Why can't you speak English?" "I can speak English," he responded coolly. "I'm choosing to speak Spanish with my friend." If you can stomach it, you can watch many videos on-line that show the violent words and fists hurled at speakers of other languages, especially of Spanish, in the US.

On a bus in Boston around 1994, I saw two men speaking to each other in Spanish. A monolingual English speaker got on, and soon berated them aggressively for speaking "their" language. With large, worried eyes, the two men silently took their conversation off the bus at the next stop. The man justified himself to the driver, "You never know when they're talking about you!" Security.

Simply the existence of other languages can elicit negative reactions. Those who accuse multilingual people of "not speaking English," do not accuse them of the *inability* to speak English, since the altercation always happens in English, but the fact that they speak a different language natively *at all*. Not only a foreign language, but merely an accent from another language suffices to anger and threaten them. They attach "un-American" values to the accent like laziness or disrespect of law and order—the "dagger" of former president Wilson's nightmare—and so justify to themselves their violent attitudes and actions.

Economic Violence

Customers Must Speak English

Within the past 50 years, we see plenty of private discrimination against multilingualism in the US and in other countries. Difficulty in communication and divisiveness form the justification for this stance, but, in fact, it arises from the effort to maintain the unnatural monolingual status quo. To squeeze languages out of the public sphere, some businesses forbid—legally and illegally—the ability to work or do business unless carried out exclusively in English, which attacks economic viability of a language.

While Americans allow others to speak whatever they want at home, they become more aggressive against languages in the public sphere, as we saw in the extreme example from Minnesota. In the 1970s, a bar in the State of Oregon created hostile conditions for Chicano patrons. Management dictated that staff was to "escort" Spanish-speakers to the back of the bar and to turn up the volume of music to drown out the language for other customers. The fear born by non-Spanish-speaking customers motivated this rule because they claimed the others might be "talking about them" in Spanish. The tavern-owners substantiated their fear by claiming that the rules were maintaining the peace between the two groups.[41] They seemed to believe that they could address "security" concerns if anglophone customers could avoid hearing Spanish. (The people in the back could still be talking about them, right?)

The federal district court struck down this rule as a violation of the Spanish-speaking clientele's civil rights. They thus established legally that the non-English speakers had equal rights to "buy, drink and enjoy what the tavern has to offer on an equal footing with English-speaking consumers." Significantly, the legal decision upheld the rights of people to speak other languages and to conduct business in them, whereby they denied the right to discriminate according to language.

In Europe, as well, some Danish tavern-owners enacted house rules, posted on the entrance of their establishments, that deny customers the right to speak any language therein except Danish, English, and German.[42] One bar owner said that he put such rules in place so "guests can have a pleasant experience and feel safe," which sounds a lot like the Oregon bar rules in the 1970s. While I recognize that these Danish restrictions began to appear after a few asylum-seekers harassed local women, significantly, the screening process to ensure "security" focused on language. Only those who spoke in one of the three languages above were considered "safe."

---

[41] Cristina M Rodríguez, "Language Diversity in the Workplace," *Northwestern University Law Review*, Faculty Scholarship Series, 100, no. 4 (2006): 1689–1773.

[42] Sara Malm, "Danish Clubs Demand Guests Have to Speak Danish, English or German," Mail Online, January 18, 2016, https://www.dailymail.co.uk/news/article-3405167/Danish-nightclubs-demand-guests-speak-Danish-English-German-allowed-foreign-men-groups-attack-female-revellers.html.

A Philadelphia purveyor of iconic cheesesteaks, Joey Vento, not long ago forced all business in his establishment to be conducted in English. He posted a sign that demanded, "This is AMERICA. When ordering *Please* 'SPEAK ENGLISH.'" In an interview Mr. Vento even stated that he discourages pointing; you have to use the English words to order.[43] After complaints by customers, a Philadelphia three-person panel ruled in 2008 that the sign did not violate a city ordinance that banned discrimination.[44] Such a sign, then, is legal in the City of Philadelphia.

As justification, Mr. Vento recounted the pressure his Sicilian grandparents experienced when they came to the US. On the one hand, he said outright that they "had to learn English." For this reason, recent immigrants should also have to learn English to buy a sandwich in his shop. On the other hand, he added, "They had a hard time. Look at the price they paid. They were limited." History attests, however, that Mr. Vento's Sicilian-immigrant grandparents likely did not simply "learn English." They surely paid a price, though, as he said, "limited" by policies like his that extracted this same price from his customers.

Let's compare the situations of Mr. Vento and his grandparents. How much English were the latter required to speak? In the 1930s, over 18% of Philadelphia was Italian,[45] significantly higher than the current 12% Latino population in the same city.[46] It would not be hard to imagine that one would have a 3 in 10 chance of hearing Italian in public conversations. They may have even been able to live most of their lives speaking Italian and may have avoided sandwich shops that denied them their mother tongue.

---

[43] Gaiutra Bahadur, "An Old Struggle to Adapt to a New Country's Ways," *Philadelphia Inquirer*, May 30, 2006, http://www-news.uchicago.edu/citations/06/060530.ngai-pi.html.

[44] "Geno's Steaks Owner Joey Vento Dies in Philadelphia," Text.Article, Associated Press, November 18, 2016, https://www.foxnews.com/food-drink/genos-steaks-owner-joey-vento-dies-in-philadelphia.

[45] Barbara Klaczynska, "Encyclopedia of Greater Philadelphia | Immigration (1870-1930)," accessed September 6, 2020, https://philadelphiaencyclopedia.org/archive/immigration-1870-1930/.

[46] "Demographics of Philadelphia," in *Wikipedia*, July 27, 2020, https://en.wikipedia.org/w/index.php?title=Demographics_of_Philadelphia&oldid=969861441.

Life dictated that they learn English, but they surely struggled not long after President Wilson's condemnation of "hyphenated" Americans. They may have been the ones pointing at items in the sandwich shop. If they felt more comfortable buying sandwiches at the Italian sandwich shop, they may have struggled communicating with their children, who spent their days in English-only schools. Even Mr. Vento, the militant monolingual, suggested that his ancestors struggled even when they learned English. Then and now, social forces crushed the attempt to conduct business in other languages, and they did not pass it down to the next generations. The grandson of linguistic violence continued the same aggression, "limiting" his customers in the same way as his grandparents were "limited."[47] Mr. Vento, like my grandmother, ended up limited as a monolingual, never having acquired his Sicilian patrimony.

Workers Must Speak English

Sixty-nine Filipino nurses in Los Angeles, persecuted for speaking languages besides English, sued their hospital for the hostile work environment targeted at them.[48] The English-only policy extended from beyond interactions with patients, to private conversations in the break room and cafeteria. Management allegedly patrolled language-use, according to the complaint, by employing "housekeepers and security guards" to follow the Filipinos—even out to the parking lot—and report back to management. Breaking this strict English-only rule could lead to suspension or termination.[49] Only Philippine languages were targeted, not the Spanish and Indian languages other employees spoke. Lawyers for the management only cited "protection of patients" as a reason for the policy. (*Security.*) The complaint was settled

---

[47] Ironically, the History of Italian Immigration Museum in Philadelphia conducts Italian classes, as of this writing. The very way we know we learn languages, from the family, was cut off, but a much less effective way, classes, came about after the language was lost in families.

[48] "Filipino Nurses Win Language Discrimination Settlement," Los Angeles Times, September 18, 2012, https://www.latimes.com/health/la-xpm-2012-sep-18-la-me-english-only-20120918-story.html.

[49] One employee sprayed air-freshener on the food of one of the complainants to register their "hatred" of Filipino food.

for nearly $1 million. Since the rule was not adjudicated, we cannot say conclusively that it was technically illegal.

Magdalena Konieczna, a bilingual-Polish and English-speaker, sued her workplace in Scotland for firing her because she spoke Polish while on the job. This business explained that the English-only language restriction was for "health and safety reasons" (*security again*) but it reached comically far beyond such aspirations. A Polish-speaking worker needed to come to a back-to-work interview conducted by Ms. Konieczna. Nevertheless, the former had to bring an independent translator; Ms. Konieczna was prohibited from carrying out the interview in Polish. Management eventually fired her. When she sued, she only garnered a small payout of just over £5,000 because she had not worked there long enough and because the court deemed her unharmed by the rule itself since she spoke English.[50] In other words, forcing someone to speak English against common sense and against their will, if they are able, does not hurt them.

These policies reveal the perception of unspoken, absurd threats. We have to protect the unfounded paranoia of bar customers who vaguely feel someone is talking about them. A single utterance in Filipino or Polish upsets someone's sense of "safety." A restaurateur protects himself from the "inconvenience" of responding to someone pointing or using an unexpected word.

Language discrimination in the workplace threatens the survival of non-majority languages; English-speakers are in no way in danger. If my children are forbidden from speaking our family language when they go to work or buy food—which people believe cannot hurt them because they can speak English—they will have no one to speak with but their own children by the time I die. The language suffocates as a British judge says that the people are unharmed because they also speak

---

[50] "Polish Woman Wins £5000 Payout after Being Banned from Speaking Polish at Work," Herald Scotland, accessed December 13, 2019, https://www.heraldscotland.com/news/14193304.polish-woman-wins-5000-payout-after-being-banned-from-speaking-polish-at-work/.

English. Whether the policies are legal or illegal, they free the ecolinguistic sphere of "weeds," to keep the English crop secure and pure.

Social Violence

American Means Monolingual

In the US, we use the term "abroad" and "overseas" interchangeably. When we imagine leaving the US, we picture crossing an ocean, even though we can drive to the countries of Canada or Mexico. American means separated by a geological barrier.

American culture imagines geography and culture as completely separating this country from vaguely defined "foreigners." Language, of course, stands at the fore. For this reason, "Speak English!" is often coupled with "Go home!" or "Go back where you came from!" even to Native Americans and Americans of Mexican descent in Texas or Colorado, whose families have lived there since before the US-Mexican border moved, and their home was taken and occupied by the US. Religion can also single one out as "foreign." Just as many sadly see Muslims today as "invaders," prominent voices feared "foreign" intervention from the Vatican during John F. Kennedy's presidency. Russian Orthodox Christians placed US flags in a prominent position in their churches during the Cold War, lest they be seen as "foreign" Communist infiltrators. To become American implies conforming exclusively, with no other affiliation, to language, religion, and culture.

Assimilating to US culture, language, religion, and so on, requires forgetting anything that does not fit in the narrow definition of "American." Of course, no single definition of "American" exists. One may simply refer to a passport, or to one's accent, to one's religion, celebration of Thanksgiving, or political party. Mixed affiliation cannot stand, as a result, as multicultural means conflicting loyalties.

As a result, multilingual means "foreign." Americans do not learn others' languages; others learn the "American" language, and their children become monolingual. Hence, a native-born citizen of the US might complain that a Latino man, speaking Spanish, "does not" speak English, even if his family has been speaking English for more generations than the family of the monolingual American. The slurs hurled against those who speak English with an accent assume that the US is not your home if you cannot speak what many claim is "standard" American English.

Some Americans would hear you speaking your native Mandarin, and then would be shocked to hear your native English and ask, "What are you?" If you did not forget your "other" language, you do not fit cleanly in what many imagine as "American." This is an old story, as it motivated the shocking treatment of the Dakota in order to "kill the Indian" and so make them American, and the violent screeds against "hyphenated" Americans who were prepared to murder our society by their divided loyalties.

A Minnesota Thought Experiment

Let us examine a common case in Minnesota. Take a small child of Somali immigrant parents and offer her a great education. Teachers speak only English. Classmates speak English, Spanish, Oromo, and Vietnamese, in addition to Somali. This Somali-speaking child needs extra help because she does not speak English. She may struggle, but our system immerses her in English, locking away any other language so that she learns English as quickly as possible.

At home, the child might be funny, diplomatic, or thoughtful with parents and grandparents. These social and cultural skills are neutralized in her English-only classroom, since she cannot communicate or understand the teacher on day one. The teacher, often monolingual, cannot access the child's talents and abilities, and does not appreciate their charge's isolation resulting from the inability to express themselves. The child with whatever intellectual and emotional capacity begins by lagging behind his or her peers academically and socially.

This child may be born in Minneapolis to parents who were traumatized by war and who never received an education in their own language. They do not speak more than a handful of English phrases, and may work hard as taxi drivers, parking lot attendants, or housecleaners. At Mom and Dad's work, English is basic and functional: issuing and receiving commands, directions, numbers. Significantly, they may have learned other languages before coming to the US, such as Swahili, if they lived in Kenya, or Arabic, if they lived in Egypt or Saudi Arabia. They are able to learn other languages as necessary to function.

The child comes home speaking more and more English. Because the school day unfolds completely in English, the task of translating that experience into Somali becomes harder and harder for the child; answers to "What did you learn in school?" become shorter and shorter. Teachers cannot communicate with the parents, and vice-versa, so both have to rely on the child to bridge that gap day-to-day. Moreover, the parents cannot convey their questions or concerns about the education of their child except through the child, and the teacher likely does not have the cultural knowledge to make correct assumptions about the student's home life. The two worlds separate more and more. No one can see the child in her entirety.

Minnesota society influences all three parties—child, parents, and teachers—to indicate that English is the language of success and other ones, of failure. The burden is laid at the parents' feet to learn English, not at the teacher's to learn Somali (just like the teachers of Dakota children, above). Rewards for learning English come quickly and visibly. The child becomes more successful at English while Somali suffers. Parents find it increasingly difficult to understand the daily life at school and the language their child spends all day speaking, not just in the classroom but on the playground and in the streets. The child spends less and less time living in Somali, and the divisions between child and parents become unbreachable.

Students' performance may suffer, since this system effectively cuts off the parents from the educational process. Every teacher recognizes that participation of parents dramatically influences academic success. As the school and social system encourage or enforce English-only, the student weakens in her native language. One modern educational researcher wrote,

> Where parents and children do not share a common language, communication is often limited to the basic

necessities, preventing parents from transmitting to their children the complex set of values, beliefs, wisdom, and understanding which provide the foundation for their children's learning and development.[51]

The connection between child and parent plays just as important a part in academic success as between student and teacher. The school teaches social skills and the important knowledge for the society, while at home kids receive love and care, as well as wisdom and values. A common language is necessary for each part if they are to come together. Without common languages, the connections essential for education become a chasm.

The student becomes more at home in English, but English does not provide her a home when her home functions in Somali. The parents cannot convey their values effectively by supporting and encouraging and disciplining her appropriately for this new social paradigm. They have disconnected. It is no wonder that officials are noticing young people, radicalized by violent organizations come from second-generation immigrants;[52] neither teacher nor parent understands them, and they are starving for a home they cannot find—even in the place where they live.

Linguistic violence, therefore, does not need to include corporal punishment. Squeezing a child so he or she cannot speak the family's native language pinches off the connection between child and

[51] Mei-Yu Lu, "English-Only Movement: Its Consequences on the Education of Language Minority Children. ERIC Digest.," Information Analyses---ERIC Information Analysis Products (IAPs) (071); Information Analyses---ERIC Digests (Selected) in Full Text (073), 1998, https://www.ericdigests.org/1999-4/english.htm.

[52] "In recent years a number of French youth—the children of North African immigrants, or converts to Islam—have become radicalized online, in prison, or by traveling to the Middle East. Such homegrown terrorists were responsible for the coordinated November 2015 attacks in Paris that killed 130 people, as well as for the shootings at the offices of the satirical magazine *Charlie Hebdo* and a Jewish supermarket." ("Liberté, Égalité, Fraternité, Racisme?," The Chronicle of Higher Education, April 16, 2017, https://www.chronicle.com/article/liberte-egalite-fraternite-racisme/.)

grandfather and even between child and mother. Without that emotional bond, the child lacks something deep at the center of their soul. Severing the emotional and nurturing bond with her parents assures the end of the language, that it will not be passed down, and depletes the home soil that nurtures her with wisdom and care.

Let us look at some ways that linguistic violence is unfolding currently in the US and elsewhere, some of which is motivated by deliberate social policy. In later chapters we will see the good side of this conclusion: as human society can destroy, we can also create space for languages to flourish.

Constructing Linguistic Barriers

Americans carry a linguistic assumption that will ultimately hold us back. As a society, we judge you based on one linguistic question: How good is your English? Based on the answer to this question, we can begin to decide on your worth as a contributor to "our" society and as a human being. The centrality of this question constructs a barrier that keeps out fellow-citizens' myriad abilities, linguistic and non-linguistic.

This system can additionally take a personal angle. For example, I worked in IT support, and our company transferred our help desk offshore to the Philippines. I spent many hours one week fixing problems that our new, inexperienced help desk could not help with. When the help desk could not help our associates, the latter called their bosses, who called me so I could offer additional support. When I talked to several frustrated associates from our company, one problem kept coming up with clear anger, "And I could hardly understand what they were saying!" The question refers to the perceived quality of their English. Then I would hear about how the help desk is broken– of which their "lack of English" was a major symptom. In fact, I had spoken with many agents, and we never had trouble understanding each other. The complaints had come from clear disdain for non-native English speakers.

One of my former co-workers is an intelligent, hard-working immigrant from Africa. He possesses encyclopedic knowledge of poetry and music from his culture, writes about the grammar of his native language in his spare time, speaks about four or five languages, and founded a non-profit organization that aids development in his native country–all without a college education. Moreover, the hardships he has endured has given him a depth of soul and feeling that I rarely encounter in people. He has the mind of a professor, yet circumstances do not allow him to develop and use his gifts to that extent. Because his English is clearly accented and he is soft-spoken, I hear frustration arise sometimes among those who communicate with him. It breaks my heart. Many of his colleagues discount him because they only hear an accent.

A French friend of mine used to work at a company, which she ended up leaving because she was tired of repeating herself multiple times when the department admin asked her questions. This happened in every encounter, and she wondered how much trouble it actually took to understand her accent. The frequency of what she perceived as unfair treatment eventually drove her to find another job. Unlike my other friend, however, she is White and completed a post-doctoral fellowship in biology at an American university.

Immigrants like my African friend are often seen as poorly educated and/or disadvantaged, in other words, lower class, while a White English native speaker with such knowledge of literature and languages would be considered the intellectual cream of the crop. At the same time, my highly educated, White, French, non-native English-speaking friend feels similar pressure for speaking the language as she does. English is not their first language, so they stand on a lower rung of the social hierarchy, either disparaged or ignored.

One may object that these barriers are unavoidable practically, as someone who does not speak, read, and write English at a high level simply does not possess an essential skill for success. With hundreds of languages spoken in the US, and written communication vital for conveying nuanced messages, we cannot accommodate everyone.

The actual reason for this "practical" concern arises from an all-or-nothing assumption. Honestly, it was not hard to communicate with those coworkers. The deep-down belief held by many Americans caused the discomfort of my colleagues; that is, if we allow one language besides English—be it German or Dakota—to hold any power whatsoever, our society is doomed.

If we can give up this assumption, we can see an enormous potential for new and renewed ideas that would mitigate past linguistic violence and offer a gift to all our people that all of our immigrants and indigenous people possess: the survival of their language to the next generation of Americans.

Community Liberties

The linguistic obituaries in the US are countless. I have not mentioned the vibrant Irish Gaelic and Yiddish communities from Europe, numerous Cantonese and Japanese speakers from Asia, and Ndongo and countless undocumented languages brought forcibly from Africa in the bodies of slaves. We have little historical documentation of the huge numbers of speakers of these languages here. While I know of my German-speaking Swiss relatives, I know nothing of the Irish side of my family. (I do not even know if they came speaking Irish Gaelic or English.) Languages come to the US to die—and to die in obscurity.

Most of the stories I told took place in the US, but this push for monolingualism infects other countries, as well. The survival of first-nations languages in Canada hang by a thread, and the monolingual impulse fuels the resistance among Canadian anglophones to learn. Mexico educates its citizens in Spanish, to the exclusion of Nahuatl and other indigenous languages, creating monolingual children from bilingual parents. All of them can kill off immigrant languages in three generations; indigenous languages seem to hold on more tenaciously, however.

What hope remains? Justice McReynolds explained in 1923 the reason why the Siman Act was unconstitutional and also the true harm of depriving children of the language of their ancestors.

> Without doubt, [the liberty protected in the Fourteenth Amendment] denotes not merely freedom from bodily

restraint but also the right of the individual to contract, to engage in any of the common occupations of life, to acquire useful knowledge, to marry, establish a home and bring up children, to worship God according to the dictates of his own conscience, and generally to enjoy those privileges long recognized at common law as essential to the orderly pursuit of happiness by free men.[53]

The Constitution's promise to protect individual liberty was thus interpreted to protect one's language as a tool by which one pursues a life within the community of one's choosing. When Meyer saw the County Attorney enter the school, he deliberated whether to continue to speak German or to switch to English. Meyer told his lawyer why he continued to teach in German: "I am not a pastor in my church. I am a teacher, but I have the same duty to uphold my religion. Teaching the children the religion of their fathers is part of that religion."[54] When the government impinges on the language one speaks in school, in church, and in the institutions and public spaces of community, its members lose the ability to educate, raise their family, and worship in the ways of their community. Cultivating multilingualism nurtures strong communities, without which their children lose their roots.

---

[53] "FindLaw's United States Supreme Court Case and Opinions," Findlaw, accessed Sept 28, 2019, https://caselaw.findlaw.com/us-supreme-court/262/390.html.

[54] Christopher Capozzola, *Uncle Sam Wants You: World War I and the Making of the Modern American Citizen* (Oxford: Oxford University Press, 2008), 196.

PART III
LOVING LANGUAGE

CHAPTER 7
SURROUNDED BY FRIENDS AND CONNECTIONS

The US is where languages come to die. My country destroys language, from the indigenous language of Mohegan in New England to Swiss German in the Great Plains. If we want to preserve languages, we must stop destroying them. We cannot simply use technology and the serendipitous goodwill and stamina of a few individuals to take on the system. The deadly system must change. When plants are endangered, we have to do more than not poison them; we must create an environment where they can flower and seed and multiply. Our entire society will have to nurture the communities that speak those languages. The battle of violence and shame waged to keep English the dominating language must transform into a network of cooperating, overlapping linguistic groups.

Perhaps selfishly, I personally want to preserve them so that I can continue to learn from and connect with fascinating people from other walks of life. I should also mention that the majority of those people appear equally excited to engage with and teach me. For example, I had read a Somali proverb one day on a bus stop, and I could not figure out its meaning, but when I asked the first Somali I ran into on the street if he could help me, he stopped to give a detailed explanation and let me record him on my phone. The more I tried to connect, the more eagerly others did so with me. These communities will not disappear quietly, though we are trained to close our ears to them.

Life's circumstances caused me to look at languages no longer as a "world" or "foreign" phenomenon from outside the US, but one from inside my own community. From high school up to my twenties, I traveled extensively and lived in multiple countries, and languages drove a lot of my enjoyment. Learning languages along the way formed an important part of my self-understanding as a traveling polyglot.

Once I decided to travel less, I no longer steeped myself in new linguistic environments, and I felt sad that language occupied a smaller and smaller part of my life. Settling on this side of the Atlantic challenged my self-perception, but the people I met in my new home in Minnesota brought me into their world. Special people gave me the gift of seeing my community in a new way, as a source of fascination that I was missing by not traveling. Discovering more about the lives of the immigrants around me made me feel at home, while they seemed happy to connect with me. Language drew me and my neighbors together.

A healthy society not only includes all languages but becomes stronger because of them. I documented my transition from world traveler to settled American in my blog, "Loving Language," from 2012 to 2017. The blog title encapsulated how I loved languages, and how they allowed me to love others. While I simply wrote weekly thoughts on language, I later discovered I was describing my transformation from "traveling polyglot" to "community ecolinguist," and my hopes for transforming my home.

The Community Welcomed Me

Mr. Somali

I started working in IT after moving to Minnesota, and a couple of brilliant Somali men soon joined our team. My teammates taught me Somali as I helped them with their business email communications in English. (My boss—a good friend of mine and admirer of my linguistic passion—teased me that I was the only guy in IT coming to work with a Somali grammar under my arm.) One of my colleagues was passionate about Somali poetry and taught me about its beauty. Over lunch we would compose dialogues of people talking about lunch in Somali. We invited coworkers to learn Somali with us.

I started frequenting Somali coffee shops to practice my language for a couple hours. As the only White person in the restaurant—or sometimes on the surrounding block—all eyes were on me. These coffee shops do not have menus; customers order the same sweet chai with or without milk. Soccer was on all the TVs, and all the men were watching. As soon as I learned how to order my breakfast in Somali, the cashier would laugh good-heartedly and any eyes that had not yet found me were squarely on me. I would eat a stuffed, fried triangle of dough called a *sambusa* (fish, my favorite if they have it, beef or lentil otherwise), and drink my Somali tea.

I would find a seat and nervously muster the nerve to talk to someone. *Would I be welcomed here? Would someone look me in the eye? Would they smile? Would they say hello?* I came uninvited into this Somali space. I sometimes forgot how to order. The language sounds weird coming out of my mouth. My skin color makes me stand out. I cannot even figure out what soccer team is playing whom. While living in Minnesota, I am foreign in this place.

They welcomed me. Once, I discovered I was sitting with my kids' school bus driver. I was so happy to learn that such a kind man was taking care of them on their way to school. On another occasion, a man a bit older than me was helping me with Somali language, teaching me some new phrases. Suddenly he looked at me and said sternly, "Don't you have a notebook or something? You should write this down!"

One arctic Minneapolis morning, I went to a café for sambusas and tea, but the place was not open despite the posted opening time. A young man paced outside, more frozen and frustrated than me. As he happened to have the phone number of the owner inside, he kept calling to pester him so that they would open. "It's so f---ing cold," he muttered to me in very colloquial English. "Come on. Let's go wait in my car." I climbed into this stranger's car and sat to wait out of the wind. When the café opened, we had breakfast together—after he grumbled at the owner.

Somalis love nicknames. Since they use a small palate of names for their children, you meet a lot of Somalis with the same ones. Furthermore, they do not possess family names; your second name is simply your father's name, your third name is your grandfather's, and so on.

So, names like Muhammad Ahmed, Ahmed Muhammad, or even Muhammad Muhammad are common. They need a way to distinguish them, so their loved ones often have a nickname that reflects their personality or physical appearance.[55] Somalis may not even learn each other's first name. My name was not important, so some called me "Mr. Somali" or just "Somali." One young man who knew another Somali-speaking White person christened me "Somali 2."

After taking a break from Somali for a few weeks, I entered one of my typical hangouts. *Waa loogu waayey?* the owner yelled at me. I was confused, and his tone intimidated me. *Ma fehmin* "I don't understand," I mumbled, big-eyed, hoping I had not offended him. His son translated. "Where were you? Where were you lost?" I was missed, and they wanted to tell me that they missed me, the White guy who spoke Somali. That was all they needed; they remembered people like me.

The White Oromo

I showed up about five minutes early to my first day of Oromo class. Alone in the class, the teacher awaited me. I walked up to him and introduced myself. "Yes. Richard!" he confirmed too quickly, and he was so friendly he surprised me. He acted strangely, as if he had already met me. I took a seat, and other students started to trickle in, until about 10 sat around the room. Surprisingly, I was the only White person. The teacher started speaking—in Oromo. Out of place, I wondered what I had signed up for.

Not long after moving to the Twin Cities, I wanted to dive head-first into more language-learning, so I looked at an adult education catalog for the local community college. They all sounded interesting—they even had a Somali class—but I "discovered" *Afaan Oromo*, a language that I had never heard of before. After some quick research I learned that it was from Ethiopia, spoken by over 40 million Oromo

---

[55] Some nicknames sound shockingly un-PC when translated. See Justin Marozzi, "The Somali Love of 'rude' Nicknames," *BBC News*, March 7, 2014, sec. Magazine, https://www.bbc.com/news/magazine-26354143.

people. So widely spoken, yet unknown by a self-proclaimed ecolinguist, it chose me.

During that first class, I caught a glimpse of the class roster: mine was, indeed, the only non-Oromo name. So that was how the teacher recognized me so quickly! Soon I discovered that the class taught literacy—to native speakers. Nevertheless, I hung in there, learning to read aloud without understanding a thing coming out of my mouth. I think the other students were just as mystified with my presence—and the sounds I was making—as I was. I met among my classmates a crew of exceptional immigrants: the daughter of a professor in Germany, the host of an Oromo-language YouTube talk-show with Oromo activists and community members, and a couple of entrepreneurs. The teacher was even the official head of the Oromo Community Center at the time. I discovered that I was the *faraanjii*, "foreigner," here in this classroom in downtown Minneapolis.

A *faraanjii* student from a previous session of the class wanted to keep practicing her Oromo. She works with recent immigrants, so she would speak Oromo regularly at work. She decided to gather us once per week at an Ethiopian restaurant. As of now, a group of us—Oromo and faraanjii—have been meeting regularly for several years. We attracted a couple more local faraanjii who lived in Ethiopia among Oromo-speaking communities. Some days we speak more Oromo than others, but we always teach about and learn each other's culture. My friends taught me about the struggles of the Oromo people and the tension they experience with the government. Sometimes other people in the restaurant or friends and relatives will stop by our weekly meetups. Through them I have met Oromo community activists, human rights workers, and an archaeologist, as well as some who were imprisoned and tortured in their home country.

After some time, I wanted to expand my circle to practice with different people. Driving on a back road in Southeast Minneapolis I saw an Oromo church. I came back on a Saturday morning to find quite a bit of activity. I went up to the front door and started asking around: "Can someone teach me *Afaan Oromo*?" I talked to a woman who took my name and number. No one called me—an unsurprising response to this peculiar faraanjii. The next week I returned, and a man introduced himself to me and I explained myself again. The few phrases I already knew maybe gave me the *bona fides* to sound like I could be serious. He promised to pass along my information to the pastor. A couple days later, I got a call from one of the church's assistants, a gentle, bright, well-educated man with a bit of time on his hands. He helped me so much to make progress and to learn about another corner of the local Oromo community.

Our Oromo friends came up with a nickname for us Oromo-learners. We were *Oromoo adii,* the White Oromo, marked by our skin as outsiders, and by our language as insiders.

Minnesota Ecolinguist: Becoming Foreign Brought Me Home

At one point, my career and my family required us to settle in one spot, but this reality did not quell my desire for travel. The longing to visit overseas, to leave my place still led me towards the languages I learned. I was not yet a full-fledged ecolinguist listening to those around me in my Minnesota home as a way to fulfill my longing.

I had already made a decision: I wanted a place to call home that was narrower than "Earth." I desired long and deep connections with others, and I wanted my kids to have the same. My wife, born in the rural US, speaking only English, understood this better than I did, as she lived in the same community of 500 people from birth until she left for college, 15 miles away. Those relationships were what I desired on the deepest level, and they drove my love of language. Tension took over my mind and soul between my two desires: substantive relationships with other people and traveling across the world, spending enough time in places to learn their languages. It was unresolvable. I simply cannot establish robust relationships as part of a community and then leave it on a whim.

Deep dissatisfaction grew in my heart, as I wanted to spend all my time with languages and foreigners. Blogs about digital nomads assaulted me, and jealousy struck deeply: I wanted to be surrounded by new people whose language I could learn and with whom I could connect—but for practical reasons I needed a steady income. I knew that I could not be fully myself if I was not speaking different languages with others. Yet those blogs assumed that one must travel to find new people, cultures, and languages. To battle my own sense of loss, I had to challenge that assumption.

Communities speak languages, not simply individuals. A person cannot know a language alone, but requires native speakers, who grew up speaking a language in a community, or at least requires teachers and textbooks, which themselves depend on those speakers. Languages die because of a loss of community. Whereas the blogs I read sought languages, I needed a community.

People make assumptions about a monolithic, White, Scandinavian Minnesota, but we live in a rich linguistic environment. Many languages have been coming from abroad for centuries alongside the indigenous ones. From Dakota and Ojibwe, to multiple East African and Southeast Asian and European languages, Minnesota offers unlimited possibilities to a language-lover. When Somalis ask me how I managed to speak Somali, I answer simply, *Waxaan deganahay Minnesota!* "I live in Minnesota!" Oromo people even call the Twin Cities "Little Oromiya."

I needed to resolve my internal tension: remaining in one place vs. learning languages. I accepted that I am not a citizen of the world; I am a citizen of the US and embrace the Twin Cities. My language studies followed suit. I stumbled into Minnesota's East African languages, and I made my home here. The longer I remain here, the better I learn these languages.

Meeting speakers of more languages, right in my community, made me curious. I opened my ears to other languages spoken around me. Having heard some stories, I wanted to learn more about what reactions these people received from English speakers, how they understood the role of English in their own and their children's lives, and when and where they decided to speak which language. For my blog several years ago, I interviewed my friends from Spain and my daughter's friend's parents from southern India to learn more about their relationships to English and other languages. Some Arab friends of mine had learned or were learning Spanish, which raised questions for me of why they put their resources into that pursuit and how they chose that language. People also told me funny stories of how their local diaspora developed new words and expressions to fit their new home; for example, Russian immigrants called the major street in Madison, Wisconsin, Mineral Point Road, "*Mineralka*." Driven by my curiosity and a bunch of new questions, I delved into these communities that lived on the periphery of my life.

I dug deeper into Somali and Oromo, which proved harder than other languages for multiple reasons. First, they are from the Cushitic language family, and so much more different from English than my other languages, even Russian. Second, I could not immerse myself in them like I could overseas; the English vortex requires effort to pull out of for even a couple hours over the course of the week. Progress advances slowly. Third, they lacked the learning materials I was used to studying with, such as textbooks, comprehensive grammars, podcasts, high-quality videos, accurate dictionaries, and—most importantly—experienced teachers. Fourth, I lacked peers to encourage me. Very few people learn these languages as adults, and my interest elicits puzzled looks from both native-born and immigrant Americans.

Learning immigrant languages, though, bears a cost because those few of us learning them do not offer commercial viability to those who might develop learning aids; I, and a couple others of us, bore the burden of our own learning. I could have spent my time learning a well-resourced language, like Italian or Mandarin, but I chose to take on this challenge.

Somali and Oromo offered an important advantage, namely, long-time relationships with my neighbors. If I want to learn Italian, I am stuck with books and occasional online conversations. If I want to learn my community's languages, I am forced to enter another neighborhood 15 minutes from my house, immersed in conversations among native speakers. While I had a limited timeline to talk to people overseas before I returned home, I could spend years and years working on a language with friends at home. More importantly, I could keep up these relationships in my community, rather than uproot myself from my friends every couple years or even months. I traded a short, intense period of 24/7 practice for slower progress with deeper relationships.

Taking on Others' Burdens

As a traveling polyglot I had faced misunderstandings and embarrassing moments that those around me probably did not even notice. As a student in France, the stress of finding my class and knowing what classes I was taking, and as a teacher in Ukraine, expressing the ideas I was paid to explain, posed huge problems that others could not even see. Sometimes I felt bullied by people who likely thought they were just joking around. Without normal verbal defenses, banter felt like a beating.

Encountering bureaucracies in unfamiliar systems in different languages frustrated and humiliated me, but also blindsided me when they arose in strange areas of life, like the seemingly simple task of buying a train ticket in Post-Soviet Kyiv. When I finally succeeded buying that train ticket, I should mention, a young man targeted me as a foreigner as I walked out of the train ticket office, terrified me by convincing me the police were after me, and scammed me out of all the cash I had on me (only $20, fortunately). The deeper I got into the culture, it found new ways of disorienting me.

As I met speakers of other languages back home in my country, they revealed to me the vulnerabilities they lived with daily. Completing tasks that I took no thought of—such as understanding job expectations or interacting with a cashier—could lead them to stress and humiliation, frustrating them and the person with whom they were interacting. Like my scammers, some dishonest people target foreigners precisely because they feel less confident in the local system. Leaving their own linguistic comfort zone took a certain amount of courage, which makes them strong.

Ecolinguism could fill a need, offering an opportunity to share their burden. Their struggles resonated with my own experience, even though their worst times sounded worse than mine. While they walked around verbally vulnerable among the local population, I, a local, wanted to make myself vulnerable for their sake. I wanted to make myself the student, the beginner, so they could rest and communicate in a way that made them feel at ease. For a moment, they could sit in a space of familiarity when dealing with a native-born American; I entered their space as a foreigner. As I longed to encounter the unfamiliar and they, the familiar, I tried to bring this experience to both of us.

Deciding Who Merits Notice

Furthermore, when we choose a language to study, we acknowledge the speakers of that language to be worthy of notice, which either further entrenches or undermines power dynamics among groups. The opinions and values of monolingual English speakers often weigh heavily in judging the worth of languages. In the Minneapolis Public Schools district as of the 2019-2020 school year, French is taught at one elementary school, two middle schools, and five high schools. Somali is taught at one middle school and one high school, and is only available to native speakers.[56] On a community level, one counted just under 15,000 French-speakers in the state, while Somali-speakers are numbered currently in tens of thousands.[57] Our society clearly did not look at the local community recently when it determined that French is worth learning but Somali is not. This determination is even more clearly shown by the fact that we do not actually know how many

---

[56] "MPS World Language Programs by Area 2019-2020," accessed October 7, 2021, https://worldlanguages.mpls.k12.mn.us/uploads/2019-2020_mps_world_languages_programs_by_area.pdf.

[57] US Census Bureau, "Detailed Languages Spoken at Home and Ability to Speak English," The United States Census Bureau, accessed January 4, 2021, https://www.census.gov/data/tables/2013/demo/2009-2013-lang-tables.html. One should note that Somali does not appear as an option on the US census, but presumably is included in "Cushite." Assuming that not all Somali speakers realize that Somali is a Cushitic language—and that "Cushite" includes all Cushitic languages—the number is likely low at 38,000. Note, also, that Hmong is not common in schools, while speakers number a whopping 55,000.

people speak Somali in the Twin Cities because the US Census form does not distinguish clearly among African languages.

The socio-economic level of a given nation or community tends to determine the interest and recognition that people give it. You probably noticed that it is very easy to find materials to learn German, but you would find (if you looked) that it is much more difficult to find materials to learn Bengali and Punjabi. Would it surprise you if I said that the number of German speakers is lower than both the number of Bengali-speakers and that of Punjabi-speakers? (German has 90-95 million speakers; Bengali, 170+ million; and Punjabi, 100 million.) Learners and creators of educational materials clearly do not pick their language based on number of speakers. Wealth makes a difference. Because German speakers tend to be richer on average than Bengali and Punjabi speakers, more people learn the former—and will pay more to do so.

Even those who learn languages as a hobby neglect those spoken by the less powerful peoples of the world. One can look on-line for people learning foreign languages, including many polyglots who speak six, seven, eight, or even more languages. Many of those who advertise their linguistic expertise, though, speak mostly European languages, and some East Asian languages. Hobbyists learn with on-line and commercial learning materials, and the materials for more "common" or "popular" languages earn their publishers more. This can explain the polyglot's tendency to learn languages spoken by richer, even if smaller, populations, especially in Europe or among the official languages of well-travelled tourist destinations in Asia.

We learn the languages of those who are worthy of notice in our eyes. *Who do I want to talk to?* They may be the rich in the most desirable areas of the world, or poorer in areas with little tourism—or those who normally pass without notice in our own communities. Once I discussed with a language-learning blogger about the language he chose to study. He decided to learn Thai, even though he lived in London, because he wanted to go on vacation there. I mentioned to him that London's second- and third-most-widely-spoken languages were

Polish and Bengali, respectively. Why not learn the language of the people you walk past every day?

Adventures in Your Community

"If you think you might want toilet paper, don't forget to grab some!"

That is what I would say when I took my daughters to visit East Africans. When I volunteered with an Eritrean refugee family, I would sometimes bring them, who were nine and ten at the time. The family used water to clean up in the bathroom instead of toilet paper, in a more African custom, so they did not always keep any around. This was the first step on my kids' adventure.

Americans normally spend time in our neighborhoods doing what is most comfortable and relaxing: barbecues with family, TV, and some occasional yard work. Occasionally, we interact with neighbors. For months, though, we can live without doing something adventuresome or vulnerable so close to home. We even crave adventure and newness, but the last place we look for it is the neighborhood where we look for constancy and familiarity.

Not only is it stimulating to put ourselves in new situations, our children's education requires it. Someone in a comfortable, predominantly White, middle-class suburb too easily assumes that most people in the world either live like them or want to live like them. They see neither what they actually possess nor what others possess who appear to be in need. I wanted to teach my children that all sorts of people are out there—starting with a 20-minute car-ride away. They live differently, better in some ways and worse in others. If we interact with a range language-communities, we will quickly find varieties of life we did not imagine or only saw in the media, sometimes within a few miles of our house.

Once, the teenage daughter of the Eritrean family was bored. "Come on!" she said to my kids. They looked at me, and I assured them it was ok. After an hour or so, they came back to me. "The police are here," my oldest whispered to me with some concern. I was alarmed, honestly, so I asked the daughter what happened. She explained with a shrug that they had caught someone for dealing drugs.

While that worried me a bit, another event left a stronger impression on my girls that day. They told me how the daughter they were with just walked into another apartment to take a ball so they could play with it. After they were done, she put the ball back. Lots of kids were around in the courtyard and outside, not just East African but also Southeast Asian. My children had never seen such trust or closeness among neighbors, even to the extent of entering each other's homes without knocking. No family was richer than another because one family's ball belonged to the whole apartment block.

When we left, the police car was parked out front. A lot of the residents were sitting outside on the stoop, calmly socializing. The scene did not look alarming at all, other than the incriminating contents of a backpack tidily laid out across the hood of the cruiser. Driving home, I called my wife: "Dear, looks like the kids saw their first drug bust today." To be honest, it was my first, too.

So much is happening not far from our homes. Other languages, cultures, races, socio-economic levels surround us, yet we manage to see none of it, imagining it far away. When we seek other cultures and languages in our communities, we find immigrants and refugees, and learn about their lives—the good and the bad. With a little effort, we can find it and show our children a bigger world, even if we never board an airplane.

Friends and Teachers: The Growing Participator Approach (GPA)

When we think "Start learning a language today!" we instinctively grab our smartphone. First, we look for apps or videos that will teach us. Second, we search for books or websites that may teach more systematically or broadly. After that, we may look for a class or a live teacher. Only by sitting down and talking with someone will we find the adventure and connection that language-learning offer.

This approach puts over 99% of world languages outside our grasp. Authors build these methods around commercial viability, and so many thousands of languages and dialects are dying off precisely because they are not commercially viable. Among the media I mentioned, videos online offer the largest range of languages—precisely because speakers produce them out of love and pride for their language. They tend to stick to the basics.

If your neighbors speak Hmong, Moroccan, or Nahuatl, these means will not get you far. Do not ignore the resource you might find online, but shift your mind to seeing your neighbors as your teachers. They hold the precious knowledge that you hope they might share.

Unfortunately, they are likely not trained to teach, and teaching one's native language is difficult for anyone. I first learned Dutch from my retired German teacher. She came from Haarlem in the Netherlands and lived all over the world, working her entire career as a teacher of German, French, and Spanish. When she began teaching Dutch, though, she was stumped. She had no curriculum or guidelines. She began our class by adapting our German textbook by writing down and cutting out those bits of Dutch dialogue with scissors, pasting them onto the German speech bubbles, and photocopying the result as our "textbook." After the tediousness of the preparations overwhelmed any joy in preparing lessons, we resorted to chatting. We would talk about languages and tell stories, and she would help me with unknown words, which I took home to memorize.

Later I learned about a method called the Growing Participator Approach (GPA), which eases native speakers into functioning as teachers.[58] When surrounded by speakers, but without materials or a trained teacher, I found that the GPA helps generate materials quickly and at an appropriate level, whatever level I am on. In this method, language-learners guide the lessons to the areas where they need more work. Knowledge of writing or ability to explain complex grammar do not

---

[58] "Growing Participator Approach," Growing Participator Approach, accessed May 9, 2020, https://www.growingparticipation.com.

play a role. One only requires some everyday objects, such as dolls and toy furniture, and some photos to begin.

The first phase instills passive knowledge. The language guide, called a "nurturer" in this method, elicits full-body responses with basic vocabulary contrasts. He or she holds up a boy doll and says, "This is a boy," then a girl doll, "This is a girl." "Show me the boy!" The learner, called a "participator," points at the boy doll. "Show me the girl!" He points at the girl doll. Then the nurturer may add a baby doll, "This is a baby. Show me the baby!" The nurturer continues to add words and objects: colors, pictures of emotional expressions, etc. Then relational words come in: "Put the boy *in front of* the girl." The participator first learns to recognize the words and react with a physical response; pronouncing the words comes later. With a smart phone, the participator can record the new words from the lesson to review until the next lesson.

In the next phase, the nurturer tells simple stories, guided by the participator. Using photos or comics without words, he relates what is happening in each. Then he poses some questions for the participator to respond to using actions. Imagine reading stories to a small child. The child loves certain books more than others to the point that they memorize the words and pages. If the story is boring or the child cannot grasp what is happening, they will pick a different one. They gravitate to the one they can learn from best.

At this point, the participator begins to tell stories of her own based on the stories learned, but also based on what the participator wants to talk about. One participator described how she steered her guide to teach her how to make Valentine's Day cards, and so she learned verbs like "cut," "draw," and "glue." Another participator, a Christian, wanted to tell biblical stories, and so used the pictures in a children's Bible as the reference. Gradually, stories progress to conversations.

The method assumes the natural link between learning languages and forming relationships. Following GPA weekly for a few months will generate a ton of material and already begins to form the bonds with the speaker of another language. Clearly, the nurturer can come from any social class or educational level; he or she only has to speak the language. For many native speakers, the exercises resemble the kinds of games you play with small children, so I noticed that elderly people enjoy the activities. I learned some Somali this way, with an elderly gentleman. He was retired and had a flexible schedule. My Oromo nurturer was a well-educated man about my age with small children. The nurturers can connect with these games in their own way, which makes the learning even more fun.

More importantly, you are learning with a person, as opposed to a book or app—the most successful method in the history of humanity. GPA explicitly functions to build relationships. If you are interested in learning not only a language but connecting with the people who speak that language, GPA works effectively. You build friendships as you learn.

Deeper Connection

I imagined a different ecolinguistic environment that reversed the English monocrop, but one in which thick, complex, healthy relationships took over. As languages thrive, children enjoy stronger mental health because of the neurological advantages of multilingualism and the closer connection to parents and relatives. Immigrants could move through life with less shame and with more support as their new neighbors took it upon themselves to connect through language. Native-born Americans would connect with everyone around them, without exclusions for language, and would open their eyes to the local cultures they would otherwise miss. Our society could become like the "three sisters" each protecting the others so that they could thrive.

In spite of historical violence, we can enrich our—and our children's and our neighbors' children's—linguistic environment by learning our neighbors' languages. We do not have to be fluent or to carry on complex conversations. Greetings, well wishes for the day, or work and family updates suffice to begin that connection. In so doing, we create space in our society for languages—and their speakers—to thrive and give license for them to pass this unique knowledge on to the next generation. Once the languages and culture flow freely in the environment, fewer obstacles prevent my children from learning

Somali, which creates more space for the language. We remove the barriers to everyone's children and provide only opportunities. I want a day when I no longer have to remind my child how different East African homes—and bathrooms—function.

These friendships healed my own disjointedness. While I loved languages and travel, I longed for community and home. For the sake of myself and my family, I could not transfer a life around the world unendingly. My immigrant and refugee friends showed me how it could be done. I sought them out, following my language love, and they generously allowed me to get them to know them and befriend them. They led me to bring together language and home.

Ecolinguism for the Whole Person

Curiosity drives my ecolinguism. I want to know how language works, how it feels, how its speakers use it, how they learn to say new things, what is most precious to them about their mother-tongue. I want to know how to form relative clauses and how to show deference to an elder. I want to stretch my head and my heart in order to connect to a new community with which I share only my humanity.

Duty also motivates me. Surrounded by refugees struggling to regain a sense of confidence in the world, immigrants navigating US government and workplace bureaucracy, I can connect with them in ways that others cannot. I remind folks like me how they can help, as I do my part as a language-lover and ecolinguist to offer a bit of ease to those struggling.

Language adventures—abroad and at home—are exhilarating! I get to feel like a scientist of languages. I love scientifically collecting data, making observations, coming up with hypotheses and testing them. For example, I tell myself, "Somali and Oromo share this word root in common." "I think I can conjugate this new verb according to that pattern." "That person's accent sounds Serbian; let me check." "That person looks like she might speak Russian." "Let me greet that person in Arabic and see what happens." "I'll try out this new grammar pattern to see if I can make a correct sentence." "Thank goodness that new Spanish word sounds just like the French word I already know."

Not only a scientist, I am an artist, creating new things, expressing whimsical thoughts, and listening to my assumptions be challenged. "How do I express this clearly?" "This word feels beautiful in my mouth." "Let me see how this man reacts when I say, *Warya!*" (A particular Somali way of saying, "Hey there!") "How do I use my Russian vocabulary to express my gratitude the way I want?" "Now that's cool! I never thought you could express that sentiment in that way in Oromo." "If I try a little extra formal Dutch, how will it affect that person?"

Connecting with another in their language primarily fulfills one's duty to serve others. It also feels good in the head and in the heart!

If you are reading this book, you must be curious about languages, too, as you see the work needed to lift up those whom others will not hear. I have left out from this book many items about language-learning that do not interest me at all, such as spelling rules, comprehension assessments, grammar tests, and fill-in-the-blank exercises. In my language-life, I minimize the importance of accuracy and maximize joy and connection. Getting something "right" only energizes me when it removes a roadblock to conversation. My curiosity drives my questions, and my questions drive my language-learning. Sometimes I learn quickly, sometimes slowly, but I always learn something, and I always love it. Now we can use that to work for the good of others.

CHAPTER 8

INSTITUTIONS AND COMMUNITY LANGUAGE

With our ecolinguistic sphere so out of balance, we can maintain hope in bringing it back. Nature wants to sprout new languages, to find new niches for old languages; she never bets all her proverbial chips on a single number.

The health and safety of our country depends on preserving these community resources. Our cities are full of Arabic and Farsi speakers, and our government declares them "critical" languages. Sadly, the children of many of those speakers do not speak either language well themselves. At most, the majority of them can discuss food and household chores; more often, they can only trade a few greetings. English crowded it out. Our social norm undermines the important goal of staying connected to the world. Had the community outside the home encouraged those parents to teach languages other than English to their children, then not only would those children be able to provide a service to our government, but other kids in the neighborhood could have learned, too. When we value the people of our community and their languages, the entire community—even the country—benefits; if we do not value them, we all lose out.

Moreover, the health and safety of individuals among our neighbors also depend on learning languages. That immigrants receive better care by health workers who speak their language comes quickly to mind. Many overlook, however, how much connecting indigenous kids to their community's languages can reverse some of the disturbing trends we see among these kids, including truancy[59] and suicide.[60] Most importantly, nurturing a healthy ecolinguistic sphere allows us all to live as we like. The Ojibwe language revitalizer, Dr Anton Treuer, wrote, "... [T]he colonizing has to stop. Most of the White folk in American forget that that their ancestors fled religious oppression and came here so they could worship and speak as they chose, not so they could impose what they brought here on everyone else."[61] As I explained above, community organizations that teach languages benefit all of us.

You can see what our communities value by what we want our kids to learn. My wife used to work as a private piano teacher. When we moved to a new town, she only needed to introduce herself a few times, and people would seek her out to teach their children. In my current town, many parents speak languages from India. Yet I have never heard a parent request on behalf of their children whether one of those Indian parents would teach their language. Playing piano is valued higher than learning one of three or four languages spoken by 100 million human beings a piece.

Small organizations, nevertheless, keep pockets of our ecolinguistic sphere healthy by reminding us of the value of these language resources. Parents often want to work to keep a connection between their homeland and their children, and so spend time with them to perpetuate language and culture. Some institutions, therefore, tend to serve only the children of those immigrant parents, so they may not have long-term staying power unless they target many generations down the line. Other institutions successfully teach young native-born Americans languages so that they can connect with various language communities at home and abroad. Both types of organizations,

---

[59] Anton Treuer, *The Language Warrior's Manifesto: How to Keep Our Languages Alive No Matter the Odds*, 2020, 23.

[60] Leda Sivak et al., "Can the Revival of Indigenous Languages Improve the Mental Health and Social and Emotional Wellbeing of Aboriginal and Torres Strait Islander People?," *TheMHS E-Book of Proceedings*, 2019.

[61] Treuer, *The Language Warrior's Manifesto*, 29.

nevertheless, keep multilingualism moving towards a healthier eco-linguistic sphere.

Language Warriors in the Midwest

Some community members decided to shoulder the difficulty of creating a space for multiple languages. Beginning by decolonizing their own people, language-restorers create space in the mind of a people whose communal language was driven out. Starting by creating multilingual space in those minds, they nurtured bilingual children, and bridged out to make their surrounding community a healthy ecolinguistic system for everyone.

The Ojibwe are fighting for language revitalization on multiple fronts. A gem in their crown is the Waadookodading K-3 Ojibwe language immersion school in Reserve, Wisconsin. Often US language schools function as "dual immersion" schools, that is, they immerse the students in English plus another language. At Waadookodading, students learn exclusively in *Ojibwemowin* (the Ojibwe language)—no English allowed.

The school does not waver in its commitment to Ojibwe immersion. At the school, even visitors are not allowed to speak English in public—only Ojibwe. If they do not speak Ojibwe, they must wait to speak until they leave the target-language space.[62]

Nevertheless, they seamlessly incorporate the demands of the State's educational standards. They focus on traditional practices, and the students learn the necessary school lessons in the process.

> For example, they take the entire school to harvest wild rice. Everything is run in Ojibwe. Everyone would offer tobacco for the harvest in accordance with Ojibwe cultural practice. If someone might ask how much rice can fit in a canoe, the older kids would measure and calculate the size of one rectangle in the center of the canoe and two triangles at the ends, do the math, and then fill the canoe with

---

[62] Treuer, 100.

water to check measurements. The younger kids would study the life cycle of a rice plant. The older kids would measure water-tension levels. They all harvest the rice, bring it to the school, winnow it, and parch it. Then they have a feast. Everyone brings some rice home to their families and learns the power of sharing, cooperative effort, and providing for loved ones.[63]

The school cleverly teaches the values of traditional work and providing for others, alongside the standards for STEM education (science, technology, engineering, and math). "Academic success" is not exclusively performed by an individual on a test, but by an entire community for the community. And teachers and students converse exclusively in Ojibwe.

Critics may wonder how well they could achieve academically in such an unusual learning environment. At a traditional reservation middle school in Minnesota truancy rates are about 50%. Test scores at Waadookodaading blow past their peers at the traditional school, who rarely meet the standard. The Ojibwe restoration expert, Dr. Anton Treuer, wrote, "Tribal-language learning interrupts truancy, and engages families and communities."[64]

Ojibwe-speakers advocate in their communities, as well. Alongside White allies, they work with community members to make the language known and visible. Public schools all include Ojibwe signage, as well as many local businesses. In a beautiful show of solidarity, local police cruisers are emblazoned with, "Ganawenjigeng miinawaa Naadamaageng" (To Protect and Serve). Dr. Treuer expressed its importance, "The signage doesn't produce speakers, but it acculturates everyone to seeing the target language in public places. That means the language isn't used just for ceremonies. It sparks curiosity. For us, it says that you're in Ojibwe country now. That's good for everyone, not just the Ojibwe."[65]

---

[63] Treuer, 141–42.

[64] Treuer, 23.

[65] Treuer, 161.

Chinese in San Francisco

When we choose to study languages, our choice testifies to our values. We want to manifest what we truly cherish. As I mentioned last chapter, certain languages more likely lead to better financial outcomes in better business contacts or job prospects. Others represent an important investment in your local community, that is, connecting with your neighbors and their history—which may differ considerably from yours.

The languages of our own communities are often undervalued compared to those outside it. Take "Chinese," for example, which consists of many distinct languages and dialects. In San Francisco, I could send my child to an immersion Mandarin school for up to $30,000 per year of elementary school.[66] Mandarin, as the official government language and most common first and second language of China, makes sense for those who hope to do business in that country. Learning Mandarin offers an entry point into the fascinating history and culture of China.

At the same time, one San Francisco public school, the Chinese Immersion School (CIS) at DeAvila, offers Cantonese immersion education. To the question, "Why Cantonese first?" the school's website responds, "Since the middle of the 19th century, Chinese immigrants from the Cantonese speaking parts of China have been immigrating to San Francisco, and while Mandarin speakers are on the rise, Cantonese remains the dominant [Chinese] language in San Francisco."[67] Cantonese is the language of southeast China, concentrated around the area of Hong Kong. Significantly, Cantonese is a major language in the history of San Francisco, which has been full of Cantonese speakers for nearly 150 years. A Cantonese-speaking community has lived in San Francisco almost as long as the English-speaking one, and you can hear more Cantonese than English spoken on the streets of Chinatown. (Notice how odd it sounds to refer to the "English-speaking

---

[66] "Tuition + Tuition Assistance," Presidio Knolls School, accessed July 25, 2019, https://www.presidioknolls.org/prospective-students/tuition.

[67] "Why Cantonese First?," accessed June 27, 2019, https://wdaes-sfusd-ca.schoolloop.com/whyfirst.

community" of San Francisco?) Learning Cantonese focuses on the current community of the city and connects with its long and deep Cantonese history.

The school focuses on heritage Cantonese speakers, that is, children growing up in Cantonese-language households. "Rather than asking Cantonese speaking children to set aside their primary language and learn English, dual language immersion allows those children to further develop their Cantonese and become literate in Chinese. This in turn provides the children of Cantonese speaking immigrants with a better foundation for learning English and other languages."[68] They aim to let children continue with Cantonese that they presumably learned at home, and to ease them into beginning Mandarin or English. That way the school preserves this valuable asset of Cantonese in the city and gives the native-speaking children a way to advance more quickly in school and to retain the benefits of bilingualism. As we saw with the 19th century Dakota children in ch. 5, beginning instruction with the home language facilitates learning English more quickly.

The school also addresses non-native Cantonese speakers when they write, "English speaking students benefit as well. By teaching Cantonese in the primary grades CIS is a more attractive school to immigrant families, and the presence of native Cantonese speakers in the classroom enhances the learning of the non-Chinese speaking students."[69] In other words, CIS offers an immersive language-learning environment wherein your children can learn Cantonese in a robust community of Cantonese speakers. Just because some kids did not learn to speak Cantonese from their parents does not mean they cannot learn it from someone else's family. For example, the son of my friend goes to his best friend's house, whose mom is from Peru. Spanish is the language of their home, so she only speaks to the friend in Spanish, as well. The community provides an essential component for producing multilingual children.

---

[68] "Why Cantonese First?"
[69] "Why Cantonese First?"

You learn a language best if immersed in a community of speakers. Many teachers of foreign languages tell their students, "You'll really learn the language once you go to the country." If from the moment I leave my front door, I will have opportunities to speak and hear the language, the amount of practice skyrockets. A Mandarin student in San Francisco can practice with speakers here and there and with movies online, but a Cantonese student can spend a couple hours living in the language in Chinatown. You learn the language you use in the community.

The unspoken question is why one would study Mandarin at $30,000 a year vs. Cantonese for free. The answer lies in what you value. Business with China—a booming economy—can make you rich, so investing hundreds of thousands of dollars in education could pay off big. Mandarin is an official government language. The Cantonese-speaking, local small business owners and workers of San Francisco will most likely not make you rich. (Business in Hong Kong, however, could perhaps earn more money.) The choice is stark: trade a potential cash payout with Mandarin for a secure community connection with Cantonese. Learning the former, you commit to communicating with the majority culture of another country; learning the latter, to associating with people in your town and even your neighborhood.

Non-native Cantonese speakers at CIS have the opportunity to integrate into a broader community; native speakers can remain closer to their family ties. Ultimately, the school explains only that a child *can* learn a language in this environment, but not why a non-native Cantonese speaker should learn this or any other language. *Any* child can become a native speaker of Cantonese, as the difference only arises from the number of hours the child is immersed in the language. If the house is constantly full of Cantonese chatter and the child must respond in Cantonese, the child learns faster. If we saw the languages of the people around us as important, our children could learn them as they grew up moving among the homes of our neighbors without a formal program, let alone $30,000 per year. Sharing our children makes us a community.

Turkish in Berlin

Nationalist and discriminatory acts in Germany are often aimed at ethnic Turks.[70] They make up a sizable community in Berlin: about 8%– the largest Turkish community outside Turkey. Many, including those born in Germany to Turkish parents, sadly feel so unwelcome that more than half want to leave.[71] Language, culture, and religion divide Turks from the dominant culture.

On the one hand, the majority of Germans remain dedicated to a cosmopolitan ideal whereby the country welcomes outsiders who are in need. On the other hand, the cultural distance between ethnic Germans and Turks brings to the surface fears that life in that country will change permanently—and not necessarily for the better.

While Germans are limited in their ability to force others to speak their language, they can always take on some of the burden and learn the language the newcomers bring. We can see an optimistic school highlighting this possibility, which is described in the article, "Reverse Integration: Germans Learn Turkish to Promote Understanding," in *Der Spiegel*.[72] This school offers Turkish lessons in Berlin.[73] They offer a brave, unorthodox way to bring communities together through languages.

The drive to assimilation constantly dominates the public discourse. According to this view, the new arrivals should leave their old ways—

---

[70] Andreas Klink and Ulrich Wagner, "Discrimination Against Ethnic Minorities in Germany: Going Back to the Field," *Journal of Applied Social Psychology* 29, no. 2 (1999): 402–23, https://doi.org/10.1111/j.1559-1816.1999.tb01394.x.

[71] "Not at Home in Germany: Almost Half of Turkish Migrants Want to Leave," *Spiegel Online*, November 20, 2009, sec. International, https://www.spiegel.de/international/germany/not-at-home-in-germany-almost-half-of-turkish-migrants-want-to-leave-a-662520.html.

[72] Kate Katharina Ferguson, "Reverse Integration: Germans Learn Turkish to Promote Understanding," *Spiegel Online*, May 31, 2012, sec. International, https://www.spiegel.de/international/germans-try-integrating-with-turkish-migrant-population-a-835653.html.

[73] "Türkisch Lernen - Türkisch-Kurs.De," accessed July 16, 2019, http://www.xn--trkisch-kurs-dlb.de/.

and language—behind to become more like "us" Germans. (Why would Germans learning Turkish be called *reverse* integration? Can *integration* only occur from minority to majority culture?) "We" will feel more comfortable that way and will not have to change our life too much. Citizens want immigrants to assimilate, to learn the "language of the country," to become vulnerable so that the citizens do not have to move out of their routines for the immigrants' sake. In reality, however, citizens cannot force immigrants to learn the language of the majority community without enacting laws and punishing people. They clearly want the newcomers to shoulder the burden to adapt; they will not take it on themselves. Those who struggle the most are tasked with "adapting" and "assimilating" by learning the language and culture, while they often work difficult physical jobs.

When we speak a foreign language, we move outside of ourselves into an area where we are uncomfortable and vulnerable so that we can communicate with someone who will be better at communicating than us. As much as nationalists would like Turks to leave, the latter have established lives and homes there. Instead of the hard work to rage against their presence, one can choose to stand beside them through the small effort of learning their language, even just a little.

Evenings and Weekend School

Since Russian is my most fluent language, I decided to teach it to my kids when they were little. Fortunately for us, the Russian immigrant parents of Madison, Wisconsin, wanted the same for their kids, so they organized a school that met weekly, either in the evening or on weekends. I signed up my little ones, so that we could all learn more about the Russian-speaking community through their language.

As a result, my kids and I would participate in the big Russian productions, like a New Year's party with *Ded Moroz* ("Grandfather Frost") and his granddaughter, *Snegurochka* ("Snow Maiden"). The kids sang songs and recited poetry to the adoring parents, just like the generation before. While my family, consisting of no Russian native speakers, confounded some of the parents, they invited us to other informal gatherings, like birthday parties, where Russian was the main language spoken.

After moving to the Twin Cities, I learned about more such schools. I made friends with a White native-English-speaker, Joe, who is married to a Japanese woman. They send their two sons to Japanese school on Saturday. Joe told me that this school requires a big commitment of several hours on Saturday morning plus homework. His family sees the value, though, when they visit Japan during the US summer break, but when Japanese school is still in session. The boys can go to class and function well, not just speaking with the teacher and classmates, but even writing their assignments.

I learned about the Chinese Language School in St. Paul, with classes for kids and adults. We also have classes for kids at the Turkish American Association of Minnesota. Minneapolis Public Schools include dual-language immersion programs in Spanish and Hmong at many schools.[74] This variety of community languages continues to exist in the US except for times of extreme pressure, such as under the Siman Act. Just like Mr. Meyer, the early 20th century teacher in Nebraska, linked language and the faith of his forefathers, modern language communities are often connected to religious schools, such as Greek children learning Greek through church, or Muslim children learning Arabic or Somali at a mosque or religious school. Their success may depend on the socio-economic class of the family, as raising a child multilingual in the US requires a lot of focused attention, not to mention half a day on Saturday and/or Sunday to take them to classes.

US Government Programs

Walking in the airport in Washington, DC, I noticed a group of high school students in matching t-shirts. I made the writing out on one of them: *National Security Language Institute for Youth*. Mixed feelings arose. "Language" *Yes!* "National Security" *Whoa …what?*

---

[74] "MPS World Language Programs by Area 2019-2020," accessed October 7, 2021, https://worldlanguages.mpls.k12.mn.us/uploads/2019-2020_mps_world_languages_programs_by_area.pdf.

This program, shortened to NSLI-Y, is run by the US State Department and declares a double purpose to "foster international cooperation by ensuring that Americans have the necessary linguistic skills and cultural knowledge to effectively communicate globally."[75] They do so by sending high school students to various countries to learn the local language through language lessons and daily interactions, as they also study at schools. Thus, they accomplish the goals of developing the hard skills of language for the US and of performing "soft diplomacy" through regular interactions.

Then I learned about another program, also run by the US State Department, called Youth Exchange and Study (YES), which sends students to countries of "strategic importance" (and also invites student from other countries to study in the US). It was set up in response to the events on September 11, 2001, and also functions as a program of soft diplomacy.[76] While students study at a school in the country, language is not as much of a focus of instruction.

In both cases, students are taught an amount of the local language and sent into the community to learn how to interact with the speakers of the language. While one understands the strategic importance of the languages of NSLI-Y (eg, Arabic, Mandarin Chinese), some of the YES countries (eg, North Macedonia, Ghana) feature languages that Americans would rarely be able to learn. While NSLI-Y focuses on national interests, YES aims to foster relationships.

The YES program encourages me as I see the US putting resources into educating American high school students in less prestigious or famous places. Learning Macedonian, getting to know Ghanaians on the street, in the community, in school make young people better. That some US Senators decided that spending this money would raise better Americans makes me feel hopeful.

---

[75] "NSLI for Youth | Scholarship to Study Language Abroad," accessed October 31, 2020, https://www.nsliforyouth.org/.

[76] "About Us," YES Abroad, accessed October 31, 2020, https://www.yes-abroad.org/about/about-us.

The Church of Latter-Day Saints

The Church of Latter-Day Saints (LDS) or Mormon Church prepares hundreds of missionaries every year, and some must learn languages for their missions. They prepare those who are going overseas to speak the native languages—not just the lingua franca. For example, if the missionary is going to Bolivia, they may be taught Spanish or the indigenous Aymara, depending on what part of the country they will live in.

This rule does not only apply to Latin America; missionaries may have to learn other languages even if their mission will take place in the US. You may need to speak Spanish or Cantonese in Los Angeles, or Korean in New York City. Furthermore, many missionaries to US cities come from other countries and so may not speak English well. They, too, will undergo language-training.

Such a skill requires in-class and in-community immersion. If you have met an LDS missionary overseas, you know how successfully their missionary system trains them in languages. I have personally met fluent Mormon speakers of Spanish, German, French, Italian, and Polish, and the Missionary Training Center's (MTC) website boasts more unexpected languages, such as Icelandic and Malagasy.[77] If you do not believe me or their website regarding their education's quality, note that the US State Department, CIA, and FBI actively and enthusiastically recruit former LDS missionaries.[78]

Community education forms the foundation of their highly successful language-learning process. LDS members believe whole-heartedly that they possess a teaching that *they themselves* should communicate to all human beings, no matter the education or nationality of their

---

[77] Danielle Nye Poulter, "Inside the MTC," accessed November 1, 2020, https://www.churchofjesuschrist.org/study/new-era/2007/03/inside-the-mtc?lang= eng. The website itself can be read in languages such as Aymar Aru and Fosun Chuuk.

[78] Sarah Laskow, "Why Mormons Make Great FBI Recruits," Atlas Obscura, November 4, 2015, http://www.atlasobscura.com/articles/why-mormons-make-great-fbi-recruits.

audience. Out of love and service for their audience, they speak to them in their language. Members of the LDS Church believe themselves primarily as messengers of the Gospel of Jesus Christ. (I am not endorsing this idea; I am just trying to reflect LDS theology.) This message teaches about love and service towards the weaker neighbor. Any human, rich or poor, is capable of receiving it. Language should not be a barrier.

Fulfilling the calling of messenger offers its own rewards because it is (or should be, at least) based on loving service. The LDS missionary conceives of his or her job principally as loving service, whether serving in New York City or the mountains of Peru. A president of the MTC wrote, "If you serve a mission faithfully and well, you will be a better husband, you will be a better father, you will be a better student, a better worker in your chosen vocation. Love is of the essence of this missionary work. Selflessness is of its very nature."[79] In the end, the missionary—the one learning the language in our case—gains by becoming a more loving, service-oriented person.

Such work reminds us of John Eliot (see ch. 5), whose religious zeal drove him to learn the Massachusett language. While not all of us would agree with the religious motivations of these language-learners, the results are outstanding. They learn languages that most do not learn, and they connect with communities most overlook. Without books or videos, they talk to people and build relationships.

Learning the language is itself an act of loving service because it enables the missionary to speak to and connect with *any* local person in this act of loving service. The local person's education or economic status does not matter. Practicing loving service in other countries as a missionary requires knowing the local language in order to connect and working on connecting makes the missionary a better person.

---

[79] President Gordon B. Hinckley, "Words of the Prophet: Forget Yourself and Go," accessed November 1, 2020, https://www.churchofjesuschrist.org/study/new-era/2002/10/words-of-the-prophet-forget-yourself-and-go?lang=eng.

I Want My Daughters to Learn Somali

In traditional societies, children grow up with the languages of the communities where they find themselves. Each community speaks its own language. If you find yourself growing up among several, you learn each language. Maybe your neighbor speaks a different language because they married someone from your town, or even your mom may come from a different place. Your paternal grandparents may speak a local language, so you have to talk to them when you go to visit.

Members of American society "discover" that those little ones speak multiple languages—and are amazed. My fellow-citizens and I struggle and sweat to learn languages. The ability of our three-year-old neighbor boy in Wisconsin to speak Spanish to one set of grandparents and English to the other is not extraordinary in most parts of the world. What is the difference?

When I walk my dog around the pond in my quiet, suburban, residential neighborhood, I pass by houses of speakers of Farsi, Russian, Somali, and Khmer. A different route includes our Rajasthani neighbors. I know I heard French once, but I do not remember which house. I have learned a little Farsi from one set of neighbors, and I can now greet the Khmer elder in his language.

Entering into the local high school, you can hear all of these languages plus a good amount of Spanish and Oromo. You might catch a little Arabic or Vietnamese.

The kids do not share their languages. At their school and in our community at large, the politest way to converse is to begin and end in English. This one language dominates to the exclusion of all others.

Once I visited an international high school in Minneapolis, which developed a special program for immigrant and refugee students. I heard little English in the halls. Many students came from Somalia and Central America, but others came from Ethiopia and China.

On the one hand, the kids clustered in linguistic groups, the largest being Spanish and Somali. On the other hand, some recognized the great opportunity of being surrounded by all these languages. "I'm learning Spanish," one Somali girl told me. "And she is my teacher," she grinned, wrapping her arm around a Latina girl.

In the family from Eritrea, I also got to know the high-school-aged son, whom I mentioned in Chapter 3. When I met him, he progressed quickly in picking up English, though his short sentences likely reflected his age more than his language ability. At one point, he told me he was learning Spanish.

"Oh! You're taking Spanish in school?"

"No."

"So how do you learn it?"

"Playing soccer."

He loved soccer and spent most of his time on the field with Central American classmates. In order to get along better with them, he was excited to learn some of their language.

In the school, these kids see each other as opportunities. No one taught them to see others this way. No teacher told them they are supposed to learn from their peers. The kids naturally thought, "Wouldn't it be cool to be able to understand what they were saying to each other?" As normal teenagers, they want to be part of the group. Language can connect them.

I want my family to connect in this same way. My kids have a friend whose parents immigrated from Spain. My family became close to them, and we love participating in parties at each other's houses. One summer my daughters stayed in Spain with their friend's grandmother, who speaks only Spanish. Even though our daughters did not feel entirely confident in their Spanish, they had to make due to keep up with the language. Because we love our friends for their large personalities, thanks to their Spanish language and culture, their daughter, who often feels the scrutiny of a society suspicious of foreigners, feels more at ease. Even though her mom and dad speak English well, they become so happy when my daughters just greet them in Spanish, and my kids feel a special bond with them.

Weekly I meet my friends at an Ethiopian restaurant to practice Afaan Oromo. (I mentioned this in chapter 7.) Since it is near the university, my older daughter will sometimes join us. The owner of the establishment is an older Oromo woman. She always greets us in her language, but if my daughter hesitates in responding, she gives her a playful smack in the arm and scolds, "You still not know Oromo? Why your dad not teach you?" These are the moms around us, happy to teach all the kids.

I dream of a society where my kids (grown now, so maybe future grandkids) could greet their Vietnamese or Somali friends' parents, or the Oromo restauranteur, in their languages. That would not mean that my daughters were studying flashcards or reading out of a book, but like those East African children, they would be spending time with their friends and "picking up" the language as children do. In so doing, they form deep relationships with people from all over the world and create more space for the myriad of cultures that arrive in the US to prosper and flourish.

Fountainhead of a New Ecolinguistic Sphere

These efforts offer hope for a healthy ecolinguistic sphere. In them, languages meet and interact inside the human brains of the community members, strengthening both the communities and the brains that house the languages. Ecolinguism requires both: healthy multilingual brains and healthy multilingual communities.

Of course, this chapter represents such a small portion of efforts and institutions around the US and the globe. Significantly, I chose these examples because they come from private individuals, private schools, public schools, government, and church institutions, targeting children and adults. While small children certainly can spare more time to learn a language—and more ego to make the required mistakes—adult language "warriors," as Dr. Anton Treuer calls them, move the effort forward. The children depend on the adults.

These test plots, islands of healthy ecolinguistic spheres offer a point of origin from which we can draw for broader a healthy ecolinguistic sphere. They slowly draw multiple languages into the public sphere. I and others like me can start to participate with a community, no longer on my own. More and more of these plots can form and be joined, as islands become archipelagos and then peninsulas. As more and more individuals participate, more families speak and live as multilinguals, and then neighborhoods and towns. These efforts can transform our society; without them, our society cannot be transformed.

CHAPTER 9
THE COUNTRY COULD LOOK LIKE...

Chaos Gives Life

Jungles denote chaos, danger, mosquitoes, and hidden danger. The jungle of Disney's "Jungle Book" is ruled by apes, and the "man-child" clearly does not belong. On the opposite end of the spectrum, North American cornfields evoke efficiency, order, and pastoral calm, like we see in the film, "Field of Dreams." What might make that wild, tangled landscape that appears so unwelcoming to humans more appealing? As I explained in chapter 6, the field cannot abide any plant or animal that survives on or competes with corn, so they are exterminated as "pests" and "weeds"; the jungle provides the means of life for hundreds of species in a robust, resilient ecosystem.

Recently I heard the heartbreaking story of indigenous people in West Papua, in remote Indonesia, who inadvertently sold their traditional jungle to a palm oil company from South Korea.[80] The people were so devastated that they could not walk past the new plantation without weeping. One man lamented, "If it's all gone, then we will be forced to live off money. Things will get worse." The plantation provided cash, but the jungle, life.

Many indigenous societies lived well for many generations off of the complex bounty that surrounded them. When I visited Hawaii, I glimpsed this bounty. I saw trees with fruit by a river, and I could just eat my fill—and there was plenty left over. Other trees produced a starchy bread fruit, which locals steam to eat with butter. Another

---

[80] "BBC World Service - The Documentary Podcast, The Burning Scar," BBC, accessed March 9, 2021, https://www.bbc.co.uk/programmes/p08y4d90.

starch came from *poi*, a pasty dish derived from the taro root. Through some gates in the streams, they could catch fish easily. The streams and trees provided all the food they needed. Now, however, large cattle ranches and coffee plantations dominate the valleys instead of an abundant, diverse ecosystem.

While the monocropping technology of the modern age offers a way to make money easily from farming, money does not necessarily lead to abundance and nutrition. In today's American corn country, people lived for a hundred generations following the buffalo and without farming. A hundred years later in that same location, where the buffalo nearly became extinct, the sweetener for Mountain Dew comes more readily than a fresh tomato or apple. The author of an article about this situation in *National Geographic* described the reality of what the people in New Guinea clearly see coming: "It's a cruel irony that people in rural Iowa can be malnourished amid forests of cornstalks running to the horizon."[81]

The simple order of monolingualism appeals to many like the square of a giant corn field. Some might think that if we do not impose the simplicity, efficiency, and predictability of a single language (English) on everyone in the US, the task of communicating will overrun our resources. In the thriving linguistic jungle, let the long-time residents of Appalachia speak their unique English and sing their traditional songs—both of which derived from their English and Irish ancestors. Let New Orleans produce blues. Let Wilber, Nebraska, (Czech capital of the USA) continue their Czech festival, and Sioux Falls, South Dakota, celebrate the annual Eritrean Kunama gathering. Maybe Guatemalans will speak their native K'iche language in Wilber, or Russians speak their language in New Orleans. The US can become the home to K'iche-speaking Czech dancers and Russophone blues artists, just as native residents of New Orleans and Wilber learn to speak a little K'iche and Russian. A thick web of languages would not come at the expense of local US culture.

---

[81] Tracie McMillan, "The New Face of Hunger," *National Geographic*, accessed November 25, 2020, http://www.nationalgeographic.com/foodfeatures/hunger/.

Just as the US created a food desert in Midwestern farm country, we have unnecessarily developed a linguistic, cultural desert in the midst of the most linguistically diverse country in the history of our planet. The human body was made to consume multiple plants and animals to function well. As hundreds of millions of children around the world show us, the human mind was made to operate in multiple languages for our brains and societies to thrive.

Obstacles

Need for Unity

A skeptic might fear that a multilingual America would drive us to a post-Babel, incomprehensible chaos. If everyone just decided to speak their own language, you would never be able to predict whether you could speak to a given stranger. You speak English, but what do they speak? Russian? Vietnamese? What if there is no common language so that the citizens can communicate with one another? US Congressperson Steven King introduced an act in 2011 to make English the official language and claimed, "A common language is the most powerful unifying force known throughout history. We need to encourage assimilation of all legal immigrants in each generation. A nation divided by language cannot pull together as effectively as a people."[82] In other words, imposing a single language on everyone ensures unity for all.

In reality, humans always discover a common language whether or not one is imposed or "encouraged." When the first English settlers came to North America, they communicated with the people there— and the indigenous people managed to get along with each other in dozens of languages before their arrival. When the Vikings came to England to settle down alongside the local Celts, they figured out how to converse—and get married. Farmers who lived along the Niger River came downstream to the delta to buy and sell; they managed to

---

[82] "English Language Unity Act," in *Wikipedia*, January 30, 2021, https://en.wikipedia.org/w/index.php?title=English_Language_Unity_Act&oldid= 1003725882.

bargain with each other. In the Old Testament, the assistant to the King of Assyria managed to speak to the inhabitants of Jerusalem in their local language (even when Jerusalem's leaders begged him to speak in Aramaic, the official lingua franca and not the citizens' language).[83]

A common language does not always unify. The English-speakers of the US provide ample evidence of that. Even if multiple peoples learn to communicate with each other, they can use that language to assist each other or for one side to impose fear on the other. A shared language will arise, but it does not ensure that they will "pull together." But without a common language, a people cannot hope to unite.

India, a country of over a billion people, manages to balance multilingualism with the functioning of a complex state. In the first tier, India recognizes in its constitution two federal languages: Hindi and English. Next come 20 other languages (e.g., Marathi, Tamil), which represent official state languages. The census recorded a further 27, each with more than one million speakers.[84] Today, therefore, the average Indian can communicate in more than one language, and some may have studied even more in school. Civilization has developed there for centuries, always navigating multiple languages simultaneously. Adeptly navigating each other's cultures and languages—not one single language or culture—unites the country.

Opponents of this vision of a multilingual US may accuse it of being a utopia, requiring more popular will, political power, and money than one person can even imagine, yet they ignore the great energy expended at this moment to continuously create and maintain a monolingual nation. The scenario we find ourselves in, as I described above, reflects the anglophone, monolingual utopia realized in the 19th and 20th centuries. Armies were mustered, a boarding school system designed, and a humiliating curriculum written for the sake of this inhumane, unjust, and tortuous end of cutting off memory and cultural

---

[83] 2 Kings 18:26

[84] "Languages of India," in *Wikipedia*, November 14, 2020, https://en.wikipedia.org/w/index.php?title=Languages_of_India&oldid=988653558.

roots. Ineffective educational philosophies developed to teach English, in fact, only succeeded in killing the home language. If we deployed one-tenth of the resources that such a miserable system requires, and with it we educated everyone and brought neighbors together, we would begin to see the scenario that I describe. In this chapter, we will see the benefits that such an investment would bring to our entire country, so that our country could bring even more value to the entire world.

Forcing a language upon everyone only imposes a power structure on a process that would unfold on its own—and we saw above the suffering this structure precipitates. Multilingualism, in fact, unites more people than monolingualism does. A shared lingua franca, rather than coerced "assimilation" to a single, exclusive language, unites nations into one people, while allowing each to continue the language(s) of their ancestors.

Not Enough Time

What if we actively engaged those institutions mentioned in the last chapter? or, at least, our children did? What if every American learned English, plus Spanish, and then an additional one like Cantonese, Oromo, Russian, Japanese, Ojibwe, or another language currently spoken in their community? Our culture would transform from one that struggles with language barriers to one that thrived thanks to those very linguistic differences.

Some might ask, "Who has that kind of time? When would those kids learn those languages? They are already over-scheduled!" The time is there. Not so long ago in the US, every lawyer and doctor learned Latin, and many, Greek. Today in Finland, all students learn Swedish and English from elementary school, in addition to an option for an additional *fourth* language.[85] They learn Swedish because of the minority of Swedish-speaking citizens of Finland. Maybe not every Finn speaks all their languages at a top level, but everyone who goes to

---

[85] "Education in Finland," in *Wikipedia*, October 22, 2020, https://en.wikipedia.org/w/index.php?title=Education_in_Finland&oldid=984904849.

school is functionally multilingual. (This has been my experience.) Singapore teaches subjects in English from the earliest grades, in addition to Mother Tongue classes in Malay, Mandarin, and Tamil (which are all official languages in Singapore).[86]

At the same time, the students of Finland and Singapore consistently outscore their US counterparts in other subjects, such as math. Thus, language-study does not seem to detract from academic success in other subjects. Two to three languages in school would serve everyone better.

Changing Communities

If we Americans are supposed to learn the language of our neighbors, we have to reconcile with one of our national character traits: our neighbors change all the time. Americans constantly move, and so do the languages spoken around me. I made friends with my Iranian neighbors when I practiced my Farsi, but then they moved away. My Marathi-speaking friend at work went back to India. I moved from Seattle and the Kunama-speaking community I knew there. The Twin Cities where I live are well known for taking in refugees. For example, after the Vietnam War, many Hmong refugees came; after perestroika in the USSR, Soviet Jews and Protestants came; after the fall of the Somali government, Somalis. As one wave of refugee ends, another begins, undermining any investment we make in a particular language.

Mastering a language takes a long time. Of course, I can learn a few pleasantries in a couple weeks, but actually conversing so that I can connect and learn about the history and point of view of these people takes years of focused effort. And I have to choose well which language, because I cannot tell you how many years it would take to learn Russian, Rajasthani, Khmer, Farsi, and Somali for the three-block radius around my house.

---

[86] "Education in Singapore," in *Wikipedia*, November 12, 2020, https://en.wikipedia.org/w/index.php?title=Education_in_Singapore&oldid=988254574.

India, in contrast, became multilingual over centuries. English itself took a couple centuries to become widespread there by colonial force, and Hindi took centuries before that. State languages each have their own story going back millennia to the early Indo-Aryan invaders that overtook a subcontinent dominated by speakers of Dravidian languages.

The US understands how to find an opportunity in an obstacle. If we get used to picking up quickly a few words of our new neighbors' language, we will become quick language-learners. You become what you do. We can become even stronger and better at new languages thanks to people's movement and diversity. Rather than prevent our multilingual development, this dynamism hastens it. In the current moment, let everyone choose what they want to speak as they expose themselves to new communities. Most will learn only basic phrases of the neighbors' languages, but a few will learn more. Most will work on only one language, but a couple will learn two to three new languages. Some people will move on, others will stay.

Some multilinguals may stay precisely because of the ecolinguistic niche formed for them where their language thrives and grows. Newcomers will actually become more at home thanks to the hustle of their new neighbors to get to know them and their language.

As people learn one language, acquiring the next one is that much easier, especially if they happen to be linguistically related. Some enterprising polyglot in the Twin Cities in the mid-1990s may have learned Somali. That person would be pleasantly surprised when they noticed a group from Ethiopia coming a few years later, speaking a related language (Oromo). After Somali, they can count to ten in the new language already on the first day! Ahead of the curve.

Languages for Our Society's Advantage

At Home

The presence of more multilinguals in the US would lighten some of the common social burdens we see broadly. When I say "multilingual" here, I do not mean that everyone would be equally fluent or native speakers of multiple languages. I consider speaking with confidence at any level—even quite basic—would help. Learning a little would help in some situations and spur one to learn more, and a little would eventually become a lot.

Poll workers and voters would be more likely to find a common language once we can reasonably assume that both participants in the conversation own more than one language, even if the vocabulary consists only of specialized terms like "ballot," "sign in," "name?" and "Where do I go next?" More people could vote and engage on the civic level, and so bring their interests, concerns, and expertise to bear on local problems.

Encounters with the police could keep both parties safer. The police could understand some basics about the person they encounter, if they can only ask where they live or explain in simple terms why they want to talk with the person. Basic commands, "Stop!" "Take your hands out of your pockets!" or "Slowly!" could ease tension and increase clarity. The work to learn a half-dozen phrases per year in one or two languages would improve policing considerably, as a couple members would take their language training beyond those phrases. Moreover, this concrete display of cultural knowledge would gain community trust as their speech projects their desire to connect with everyone.

If every doctor and nurse were required to be competent in one other language, plus master key phrases in a few more, improved rapport would result in more people having access to life-saving treatment. Just simple phrases like "Where do you hurt?" "How long has this hurt for?" can help a doctor connect and begin a diagnosis. I once assisted a group of US doctors visiting Ukraine as an interpreter. An elderly patient complained of headaches and dizziness. The doctor asked, "What medication do you take? Can you please show me?" As soon as I interpreted, the woman pulled out a shoe box of medications. That was all the doctor needed to determine that her symptoms likely came from her medication. He only required two questions. If the professional feels comfortable conversing in another language, we could assume that their comfort surely came from deeper interactions with another community, which means that they could administer healthcare with more intercultural competence. Treatment could improve.

If every teacher could converse in another language, the act of acquiring that language would remove huge obstacles as they understood better some of their students' impediments to learning. While students might know enough English to get the general conversation, teachers could clarify certain details such as dates, page numbers, or test days—which are a challenge for a student who does not share a native language with the teacher. If the students were learning each other's languages, individual students would likely run into fewer obstacles following a class lecture; other students could help.

Learning a language helps empathize with others learning a language. You know the roadblocks, such as missing an important word or two. For example, I experienced countless times someone speaking to me in a language where I could almost—but not quite—understand what they were saying. I missed a word (or two?). When I said, "Please repeat," they would start over and try to say the same thing in different words. While they thought they were aiding my progress, I was back at square one, stuck on a couple additional new key words. As a result of my experience with other languages, I treat non-native speakers differently than others do. I try to repeat myself word-for-word with English speakers who do not understand me because I know that their problem likely arises from not hearing just a couple words.

We could also unleash fantastic skills among Americans by removing impediments to re-licensing immigrants. I have met brilliant Ethiopian lawyers, Russian doctors, and others who have no way of practicing their valuable knowledge because of limited English. The US is losing out, as many skilled engineers and scientists are driving taxis because monolingual managers cannot listen past their accent in a job interview. If someone wants to teach a language in school, they must pass a teaching certificate exam in English, which ironically may exclude the best candidate for teaching the foreign language. If the person lives in the US anyway, widespread multilingualism will ensure that society benefits from every newcomer's entire life of experience and professional knowledge.

A multilingual America offers services, engagement, safety, and talent for everyone. Americans would welcome new immigrants more readily and speedily, which would help along the process by which they learn about the people and culture of the US. More enthusiastic immigrants who are more engaged in society—from voting, to receiving health care and practicing their professions—generate a safer, more creative, and more dynamic society.

Overseas

A more natural ecolinguistic sphere, rather than our monocrop of English, would benefit our society's relations overseas. The Arab world during the Middle Ages offers an important example where a single lingua franca not only did not squeeze out other languages, but the whole society benefitted from linguistic diversity. Starting in the 8th century, an Arab elite ruled most of Spain, which they called, "Al-Andalus." The city of Córdoba (Arabic, *Qurṭuba*) sat at the center of culture for most of the world, as we might think New York City or Paris does today. The common language of speech and writing was Arabic, and it followed the literary paradigm established by the Muslim holy book, the Qur'an. As a result, educated people spoke and wrote in Arabic.

At the same time, minorities functioned in other languages. Jewish thinkers wrote in Hebrew, and Christian scholars were proficient in Latin and Greek. We also have evidence that people spoke other languages in and around Al-Andalus, such as Basque and dialects of the Vulgar Latin ancestors of modern Spanish (Castilian) and Catalonian. People performed different functions with their languages. For example, the Jewish philosopher Maimonides wrote important philosophical and theological texts in Hebrew for global Jewish consumption, whether in Spain, France, Italy, or elsewhere, and in Arabic for Jewish and non-Jewish readers inside the Arab sphere of influence.

Rather than try to stamp out minority languages, the Arab rulers decided to capitalize on these resources. When sending envoys to neighboring countries, such as to Paris, they sent Christians, fluent in both Arabic and Latin. When making business deals with Venetians, they counted on the linguistic and family connections of Jewish residents. When Arabs wanted broader access to famous philosophical texts, such as those of Plato and Aristotle, they counted on Christians to translate these texts into Arabic. Jews helped translate the Hebrew Bible (Old Testament) into Arabic, as well. What we would call "think tanks" of Andalusian translators worked in Córdoba to produce important works in Arabic. The multicultural population of the empire was nurtured for many centuries in order to provide a bridge to connect the general population across global culture.

Even the US provides examples of how a complex ecolinguistic sphere helps the country. During World War II, Navajo-speakers conveyed messages for the US Marine Corps in the Pacific theater. Referred to as "code talkers," one Navajo person would speak to another over a radio to communicate in an unbreakable code. Other Native Americans performed similar tasks, and all helped out the US precisely because they spoke the English lingua franca as well as another language.[87]

During the same period, the US military intelligence in their fight against Nazi Germany recruited refugees, especially German Jews, specifically because of their linguistic and cultural knowledge. Known as the "Ritchie Boys," these people understood the language and mentality of the enemy, so they carried out interrogation and counterintelligence. Not only did this unit work in the German language, but also in French, Italian, Polish, and others.[88]

If every soldier deployed to Iraq learned Arabic or if to Afghanistan Dari and Pashtun, relations with locals would surely improve. Maybe the US government would employ LDS linguists to teach. Training a soldier in a couple months would surely resemble preparing missionaries.

---

[87] "Code Talker," in *Wikipedia*, March 16, 2021, https://en.wikipedia.org/w/index.php?title=Code_talker&oldid=1012373491. Ironically, the plan came together only because Philip Johnston, a White Navajo-speaker whose missionary family grew up among the Navajo, proposed it to the military.

[88] "Ritchie Boys," in *Wikipedia*, March 7, 2021, https://en.wikipedia.org/w/index.php?title=Ritchie_Boys&oldid=1010815334.

We could do much better than simply fill the military with languages. If we cultivated a rich ecolinguistic sphere, full of complex relationships, we could fill our US State Department with multilingual people. International government posts would eventually require multilingualism and draw from a diverse pool of linguistic experience for any interpersonal or multi-cultural work overseas. Diplomacy could be carried out in any language, with the English lingua franca used only in specific, multinational cases. We could continue to work in an English lingua franca environment, but the additional languages and cultural expertise would expedite good outcomes.

Any company could also hire with a diverse pallet of language talent. Currently, companies work hard on "localizing" their product, that is, making it ready to sell and market in other countries. If the marketing divisions of global companies could fill its ranks with people who could explain the target country's culture and mentality—just as military intelligence did with the Ritchie Boys—this project would be much simpler. Once the US used these resources properly, US companies would find they held a huge advantage over the mono- and bilingual competition.

Languages for Our Children's Advantage

Healthier Brains

We speak the language of those closest to us, but we speak other languages for other purposes, like trade, religion, or socializing. We know that multilingual people more than monolinguals retain their language faculties more often after a stroke and knowing more languages leads to less devastation from Alzheimer's Disease.[89] While some experts disagree, many studies have noted that knowing more languages helps with executive function and problem-solving

---

[89] Ellen Bialystok, Fergus I.M. Craik, and Gigi Luk, "Bilingualism: Consequences for Mind and Brain," *Trends in Cognitive Sciences* 16, no. 4 (April 2012): 240–50, https://doi.org/10.1016/j.tics.2012.03.001.

abilities.[90] Many advocate the cognitive benefits of multilingualism for children.

If we flip from the assumption of a monolingual norm to a multilingual one, however, the view changes. Claiming that multilingualism is a "benefit" imagines a world where "adding" a language is optional, that by default children would "remain" monolingual. We assume that you must *do* something for a child to become bilingual. Yet a large portion of children steeped in multilingualism worldwide acquire languages, and we can imagine, as I mentioned before, that before the rise of nation-states, an even higher portion of children were multilingual. Humans evolved for multilingualism, as evidenced by the multilingual benefit.

The correct question is not, "What happens when we add a language to a child's repertoire?" but, "What happens when we limit a child's linguistic input to one language?" When we restrict a child's input, we impoverish their brain. Our monolingual environment exposes them to cognitive danger and risk: higher risk of debilitating Alzheimer's, less resilience after a stroke, and potentially lower cognitive abilities. We could ask the question, "What happens to a child's body when nutrition is limited to chicken nuggets?" but no one could get funding for such an abusive experiment. The child's body would suffer from malnutrition. Just as limiting the same child's nutrition to chicken nuggets every day will impede their body's development, restricting their brain's linguistic input to one language stunts their brain's health.

Monolingualism is hazardous to the health of adults and children. Let's give them the nourishment they crave.

Connections Overseas

Once these young people talk to their classmates about what they read and hear, along with a little of the language they heard it in, those

---

[90] Ed Yong, "The Bitter Fight Over the Benefits of Bilingualism," The Atlantic, February 10, 2016, https://www.theatlantic.com/science/archive/2016/02/the-battle-over-bilingualism/462114/.

speak in turn to their relatives and parents, and soon Americans become worldly, aware, and nuanced thinkers. Europeans would no longer laugh at Americans for mixing up Serbia and Siberia and Syria, or for believing that the Republic of Georgia sits atop Florida. No one would remind Americans that Africa is not a country, as they could discuss the differences between Nigeria and Namibia. Americans could master language and world events easily—and one day be accused of their "unfair advantage."

When all of this finery stands in front of us all the time, children become multicultural because the US expects it. So-called "insiders" would not view the complexity of "outsiders" with suspicion; simplicity would no longer exist.

If kids in my suburb kept a strong linguistic tie to the country of their ancestors, my children could mingle with those deeper ties to India, Ethiopia, and Vietnam, among others. The school would not fly flags of the countries from which families came from; everyone would be American, in the most multilayered way conceivable.

New friends could listen to Grandma tell about how the young man courted her sister growing up in Ethiopia back in the day, even if she does not speak English. Or to Uncle tell the stories in the language of his grandfather, who still remembered wild buffalo in South Dakota. Their knowledge, wisdom, and experience would enlighten a new generation of their grandchildren—both biological and communal.

Killing languages cuts ties overseas, so a multilingual US could unite countries around the globe rather than sit in isolation, on either side an ocean away from the "old world," while we all stay connected with those people who dwelt in North America for a hundred generations before. Each community could remain in touch with the relatives and friends, and children continue to communicate with uncles and cousins in whatever language they always did. Even more, new friends in a new country could begin to connect with family and friends back in the "old country." Language learned and used in the new country among our complex communities would facilitate new relationships in new countries, thickening the web of friendship.

The US would no longer feel isolated, as all Americans would hear from their neighbors and friends the daily goings-on in the Middle East and Sub-Saharan Africa. They would not just count on the media for the "newsworthy" events, but by hearing their neighbors and becoming familiar with languages, they would know actual, daily life. When needs arose in those places, connecting would be easy. Already, we have the advantage of modern communication technology. Let us move ahead of slow-moving translation technology, limited to only the most commercially viable languages, to speak and text directly with our new friends across the ocean. As I mentioned above, my Somali friend in Minneapolis was moved to join with his friends to help drill a water well in a remote area of his home country. While a traditional US NGO staffed by native-born, European-descended Americans, such an undertaking would have required months of travel and planning. Thanks to my friend's language skills, he and his friends organized it all over the phone in a few weeks. If my children learned Somali from his children, they could work together to drill the next generation of water wells. Through more language competence, we could learn what their needs are so that we could take advantage of the opportunity to serve, not by imaging their needs, but by actually hearing it from the one in need.

Multilingualism Ensures Multiple Points of View

Precisely because the US attracts bright, tenacious, driven immigrants from every country in the world, and is home to multiple indigenous peoples and descendants of immigrants, their different cultures and points of view give the US its strength to innovate and attract such people in the future. By promoting and requiring multiple languages, our society would increase in creativity and productivity.

Multilinguals navigate not only languages, but also the communities that speak them. By learning how to function in different social spaces, speakers of both languages offer special gifts for solving problems in new ways.

Every culture in the history of the world has dealt with internal and external conflicts. India and Indonesia face the challenge of bringing huge varieties of people together, and Poland and the Democratic Republic of Congo have survived multiple rounds of being someone else's strategic foothold. Each one developed original ways of dealing with disputes and tension.

For example, the US faces, as a country and millions of times a day on a small scale, problems to solve among people of the same and different groups. The US possesses a palate of methods for problem-solving and conflict-ending on both the international and domestic fronts. Those who can communicate those novel methods to the broader society must possess multilingual and multicultural competence, and the one who learns from them will produce new ideas more quickly in peace.

As someone who has worked in IT for many years, I have seen the growth of multicultural teams. Members may be US-born, foreign-born, and living either in the same country as me or in another one. I have worked with Filipinos in Manila, Somalis in my town, Germans in Germany, and Indians in the US and in India, just to name a few. Working towards a common goal makes communication the most important part of the team, by which its common success rises or falls.

One study found that multicultural teams saw the most success when they openly recognized the differences in cultures on the team—and then worked around and through them as a team. Only if this did not improve the dynamic, did they have to change the team makeup, or to bring in management to set expectations or even remove someone from the team.[91] The most productive, equitable solution came about when everyone on the team negotiated the cultural differences together openly.

In the realm of cultural differences, the presence of a multicultural individual can significantly raise the effectiveness of original solutions that the team produces. Moreover, the person does not even need to share a culture with the people on the team; simply the fact that the

---

[91] Jeanne Brett, Kristin Behfar, and Mary Kern, "Managing Multicultural Teams," *Harvard Business Review* 84 (November 2006): 84–91.

person navigates adeptly between cultures allows a team to outper-form teams of monocultural individuals by roughly 28%.[92] These cul-tural "brokers," who can elicit and integrate knowledge from different cultures, catalyze teams to work more intelligently and creatively.[93]

While multicultural teams are our modern reality, and they potentially create better solutions than monocultural teams, one must manage them carefully.[94] If people are willing to work through cultural differ-ences, they will thrive. If at least one team member is multicultural, they can improve the team's success even more. Without one of those two elements, multicultural flexibility or experience, the team will more likely require intervention from management or even dissolution of the team. As frustrating as they can be, cultural differences are worth working through.

When more languages enter into the public sphere and work environ-ment, we hear more voices and more multicultural individuals can rise to the occasion of brokering solutions to our most difficult issues. When all are multilingual, few teams will ever lack a cultural broker who can bring voices together into singular, innovative answers and solutions to difficult questions.

These dynamics in large companies lay out a paradigm that our whole country can emulate in various ways. When every American global corporation brings the voices of its international customers and asso-ciates into the decision-making process in their native languages, companies will enjoy a new level of innovation—as well as more le-gitimacy around the world. Imagine how those outside of the US view American "multinational" corporations, where the leadership is able to converse exclusively in English, and an American point of view enjoys complete hegemony. Our social institutions can follow suit—

[92] Adi Gaskell, "How to Build Successful Multicultural Teams," *Forbes,* July 18, 2018, https://www.forbes.com/sites/adigaskell/2018/07/18/how-to-build-suc-cessful-multi-cultural-teams/.

[93] Sujin Jang, "Cultural Brokerage and Creative Performance in Multicultural Teams," *Organization Science* 28, no. 6 (December 1, 2017): 993–1009, https://doi.org/10.1287/orsc.2017.1162.

[94] Gaskell, "How to Build Successful Multicultural Teams."

and enjoy the same prestige. Once multilingualism is the norm, our companies and our communities have access to rich *renewable* veins of creativity to mine in the US and abroad.

The Unfair Advantage of the US

Once Americans broadened the profile of an "American," we would introduce to the public sphere beautiful displays of language and culture, religion and history. We could learn about and connect with the world, as we spoke to them, word by word, phrase by phrase, in their languages.

Our society would perfect the art of learning the next language, of hospitality, of connecting with the new neighbors. With such a rich ecolinguistic sphere, languages would stick. Members of the original transplanted community might leave, but the language might even remain after they left, as the new learners and the young generation speak it in their daily life.

Education, business, politics—all would flourish with a foundation of connection and understanding. Socially, we would understand each other, and globally, we would understand the world. Even our brains would regain their natural health as the ecolinguistic sphere became a balanced, rich environment, rather than the sickly, violent monolingual monocrop that has existed here way too long. The US would gain a resounding advantage for producing the best linguists, world affairs experts, and diplomats.

The US appears as an isolated, anglophone country, but politicians have manufactured both traits. The assumption of Rep. King, above, that forcing a single language in our public life unifies, expresses the ideology that created our linguistic insulation. With our nation's immigration policy and distance from most countries, it lives on its own. Nevertheless, we, as Americans, imagine ourselves as a "nation of immigrants" or "established by immigrants." While this conviction erases the indigenous population of the North American continent before Europeans, Asians, Africans, and South Americans streamed in, it represents the dominant, hegemonic narrative.

As the descendants of immigrants, of chattel slaves, and of displaced victims of genocide, we became isolated from our ancestors when our society annihilated the memories, connections, and languages we held in common with them. Imagining ourselves as a nation founded by immigrants, we are immigrants no more. Hence, we pay homage neither to the nations that lived here before us, nor to the "sending" nations that supplied the foreign population. At one gauzy time in history we were *e pluribus* "from many," but now we define ourselves as a monolingual *unum* "one." We have been cutting every would-be American off from our roots for generations by suppressing and killing the languages of the people who came before us, in the New World and the Old. Our society can embrace that even today, not just in history, we come *e pluribus,* and that shared variety makes us *unum.*

PART IV
LOVING LANGUAGE

CHAPTER 10
VULNERABILITY

When we learn community languages, we lean into our own and others' vulnerability, which results in richer, wholehearted relationships, among individuals and communities.

In the last section, I described how precarious life is for speakers of other languages. Cultures like that of the US eliminate and kill off languages through what we euphemistically call "assimilation." It is not enough to force everyone to speak English by coercing everyone to raise their children as native English speakers. Our culture forces assimilation to the point of preventing natural multilingualism and aiming suspicion and even punishment on speakers of any language besides English. Any language but English in the public sphere can elicit animosity.

Before we worry about "sounding dumb" in the language we choose to learn, let us remember the daily situation non-native speakers of English experience in the US. If you do not speak English as a native, your accent makes you vulnerable. An incorrect word at work can jeopardize your job, on the bus can get you lost, at the store can result in insult, and during a police stop can risk your freedom or life. This is why Amy Chua wrote, "Do you know what a foreign accent is? It's a sign of bravery."[95] That person left everything they knew so that they could live this life in spite of their vulnerability.

Getting used to that route to vulnerability provides all sorts of advantages. The vulnerability of speaking a language poorly that might not be well received, that might make us sound dumb, is not weakness, we will find. Dr. Brené Brown, a well-known TED speaker and researcher on shame and wholehearted living, wrote, "Vulnerability is

---

[95] Amy Chua, *Battle Hymn of the Tiger Mother* (The Penguin Press, 2011), 86.

the birthplace of love, belonging, joy, courage, empathy, and creativity. It is the source of hope, empathy, accountability, and authenticity. If we want greater clarity in our purpose or deeper and more meaningful spiritual lives, vulnerability is the path."[96] Speaking a language well means speaking badly for a long time, yet it is a vehicle that will keep us on that path to wholehearted living. All the time we speak it badly we gain a deeper experience of life as we connect with others.

Dr. Brown also wrote, "I define vulnerability as uncertainty, risk, and emotional exposure."[97] Every language student—in class, on the bus, or at the police station—has experienced all three of these. Rather than diminishing us, speaking the language makes us deeper, braver, and hopeful. How much better when we connect with another person in that moment of vulnerability!

We meet that person in our shared vulnerability. They are vulnerable every day; we make ourselves vulnerable in their language so that just for one moment, they are less vulnerable. We can meet them where they are at by learning their language. Soon, our experience will show us how well they speak English. Our attempts at connecting with them in their vulnerability will teach us and offer a hand to our new friends.

Eight Ways You Might Be Linguistically Privileged

One time I was watching a video of an American woman visiting Spain. She met some locals, and they started a conversation. After a few awkward laughs, one of the locals furrowed her brow.

"Ehhh…I sorry. My English…ehh…not so good."

"Oh, no!" the American intoned slowly and deliberately. "Your English is just fine! It's way better than my Spanish. You're doing great."

By her compliment, she just shifted the burden of speaking a foreign language off of herself to a person who is in their home and who

---

[96] Brené Brown, *Daring Greatly: How the Courage to Be Vulnerable Transforms the Way We Live, Love, Parent, and Lead* (Penguin UK, 2013), 37.

[97] Brown, *Daring Greatly*, 37.

expressed their insecurity in speaking. I feel like I have seen this scene repeat over and over. The local struggles with English to communicate with the US guest, and the American, without taking on any of the burden, encourages them to continue to struggle. The exertion takes energy and concentration—exhausting. At best, the conversation will end with a nice connection. Without question, the speaker will second-guess if she sounded stupid or if she even said what she intended to say. She likely will feel embarrassed at some point during the encounter.

The American can smile and drink her wine, too embarrassed to recall her high school Spanish. The Spaniard exerts herself for this visitor, too embarrassed not to exercise her high school English—and focusing too hard to even think about finishing her drink. Many of us native English-speakers do not recognize the privilege that we enjoy, but when we compare our daily experiences to non-native English speakers, the differences put these advantages on display. Let us consider eight such facets of this linguistic privilege.

First, we verbalize our feelings without a problem. For example, we enjoy joking around with our coworkers. My friend from Madrid who immigrated to the US, laughed about how she cannot tell jokes at work: no one thinks they are funny. She tries to explain them, making them even less funny. In another instance, when I got angry in Morocco and tried to convey my emotions in Arabic, people either laughed or tried to calm me down like I was a child throwing a tantrum. I could not articulate my frustration as a mature adult. I could carry on a conversation, but I could not express my feelings.

Second, I have a ripcord as a native English-speaker if I run into linguistic trouble. I am allowed to ask another person if they speak English when I get frustrated. A Russian- or Amharic-speaker in Minneapolis cannot ask if the other person would kindly stop speaking English. No Hispanic even has ever asked me if we could change over to Spanish, in spite of the fact that many Americans study Spanish as a second language.[98]

---

[98] Only once in the US did someone ask me for directions in Spanish, but that

This example of linguistic privilege goes only to anglophones: I can ask for someone who speaks my native language literally anywhere in the world. We measure remoteness and civilization by the ability of local people to speak English. If I go to a village in western China, the mountains of Armenia, or the islands of the Maldives, I can expect to find someone who speaks my language. In the story of the Kurdish refugees that I told in chapter 1, it was not surprising that one person in their party spoke English. Some monolingual anglophones even assume that someone *should* speak English. A friend of mine traveling in Greece once overheard a young American tourist complain to his companion, "… and they didn't even have the *common decency* to speak *English!*" Contrary to his belief, these speakers of other languages exhibit politeness to us by speaking our language; it is decent to return the favor, even a little bit.

Third, with a little deference and charm, I can amicably walk away from a police stop. Someone who does not speak English as a native cannot always hit the emotional buttons he or she would like to or pick up on nuances that the officer may be conveying. I never worry that a misunderstanding could end my life.

Fourth, people around me in my home do not pose a mystery; I know exactly what they are saying. As a native English-speaker I can pick up on bits of words and phrases and put together a meaning that allows me to grasp what is going around me. When you do not know the language well, you feel more disconnected from or even suspicious of your surroundings. I studied Russian in college, and many of my classmates were immigrants from the former Soviet Union. Feeling disconnected, I pictured in my mind their intelligent, funny conversations and longed to be able to follow what they were chatting about in the cafeteria and the hallways. Once I mastered Russian, I began with interest to eavesdrop on what they were saying:

"Hey! What did you get on that test?"

"An A."

---

was in Miami, which is the closest to a bilingual city as I have seen in this country.

Or,

"Sasha, are you going to the party tonight?"

"No, I have to study."

Sure, these conversations—neither intelligent nor funny—completely disappointed me, but I was directly experiencing reality, no longer living a mystery.

Fifth, you learn much faster studying subjects in your native language. When the teacher and textbook present the material in a foreign language, you read more slowly, and you do not grasp some details of what the teacher is saying. I had always studied my way to the top two students of every language class I took. My first semester of Ukrainian history in Kyiv, however, tormented me. The professor lectured in Russian—hard enough—and I had to slog my way through a textbook in Ukrainian, which I had just begun to learn. Someone could, of course, say to me, "Learn Ukrainian! It's the national language, you know!" as many do about English in the US. I truly struggled because I wanted to learn. The most difficult class in my life assumed advanced knowledge of the other language.

A good friend of mine, whom I studied with in the US, does not speak English as her native language. She learned well; she expressed herself and comprehended English great. The subject matter—Hebrew—challenged her especially. She ended up studying twice as hard as the rest of us to learn the same thing in our native language. She wrote her dissertation in English, too, of course. While the degree ascribed the same letters after her name as that of our other classmates, her perseverance and extra work earned her even greater respect.

Sixth, when I tell my kids something important, they know exactly what I mean. My words may surprise them, but they never land with an expressionless thud. I have a friend who speaks excellent English, but she reprimands her children in her native Mandarin. Sadly, though, they do not speak Mandarin. They cannot communicate with their father, who never learned English at all. In another example, I heard a story recently about a child whose family came from Haiti, but who struggled to connect with her mother about some success or award at school because the daughter spoke English and the mother, Haitian Creole.[99] The many children in the US growing up with grandparents who speak only Nahuatl or Cantonese repeat the sad history of broken ties that the grandchildren of Cherokee and Mohawk experienced.

Seventh, I conduct business from different angles and with shades of meaning that I do not possess in a language other than English. People took a long time teaching me how to bargain in Morocco and Ukraine, and I never succeeded much. Since I was richer than the average in both of those countries, I did not suffer terribly. My friend from Somalia, however, struggled in some seemingly simple situations. For example, he often felt cheated when he got his car worked on, as the price was always changing in ways that confused him. (He resorted to paying for a lawyer service who spoke or wrote letters on his behalf when he felt that business-owners treated him unfairly.)

Eighth, I can choose not to study a foreign language (even though it is completely against my nature personally). Schools in the US and UK lament how few students study foreign languages, and of those, how few can speak the language competently, yet education requirements are slow to change. Any of our citizens can declare themselves "not a language person," and society places no more expectations on them to learn. If my language were Lakota or Pitjantjatjara or Estonian, however, I would have little choice in learning a foreign language. Depending on my local community, studying a foreign language may affect my personal economic status as much as reading and writing. Acquiring a charming pair of greetings in English would not ingratiate me to anyone; I would have to learn English well or be significantly excluded from a huge portion of society.

When you listen to that person in your community who speaks with an accent, recognize the privilege you possess. When you feel embarrassed to speak a few words of Spanish or to pronounce a difficult

---

[99] Katiana Ciceron, "The Cultural Wall," *The Moth,* accessed December 8, 2022, http://themoth.org/dispatches/storytelling-school-the-cultural-wall.

Indian surname, think of those around you who cannot get out of this challenge so easily. (Ask any non-native English speaker who is expected to pronounce the difference between "Brandon" and "Brendan"!) You can spend some of your privileged linguistic inheritance on learning a language from your community, so that even for a short moment, your neighbor can experience just a moment of decency, of kindness, and of privilege.

This privilege can run against other sociological categories and intersectionality. A Black American speaks English as their native language, while a White Moldovan might barely speak a word. A born English-speaker who dropped out of school may understand a letter from the IRS that a well-educated physician from Iran cannot. Simply growing up with a majority language offers us a whole slate of privilege that we must recognize.

Empathy through Struggle

By choosing to learn a community language you voluntarily give up your privilege. You remain at home but place yourself in the position of ignorance and childishness. Conversely, the person you speak with gains the position of power, where he or she grasps what is being discussed better than you.

As you grow in frustration, you can imagine the everyday feeling of those who do not speak English as their native language. Many immigrants move through their day getting on a bus unsure of whether it goes where they need; talking to teachers unsure of how to help their children succeed; visiting the doctor unsure if they really explained their problem accurately; leaving the DMV unsure of why they failed to get their driver's license. They only know that they did not grasp everything the other person was saying—and wonder whether they got the most important parts. While understanding much of your new language, you share this frustration with those you are talking to.

Maybe you can extrapolate another level out to the lives of serial immigrants. While you struggle with every phrase of the language you are learning, taking on an additional one may seem superhuman.

Many immigrants, though, spent time in multiple countries and became accustomed to acquiring an additional language in each of them. My friend's father immigrated from Yugoslavia to Australia to Canada. When my friend was having trouble communicating with a francophone Canadian, his father grabbed the phone and surprised my friend by speaking with the person on the other end—in French, which he had picked up along the way.

A Somali friend of mine left his country for Ethiopia. Soon he found work as a Somali-Amharic interpreter, before he left for Chad and then Mali. When I met him, he had forgotten most of his Amharic, but still spoke the French and Bambara he had to learn to finish school in his new countries. In the US, he not only learned English, but we worked together in communications.

I volunteered to help a refugee family from Eritrea. The family knew their native Kunama, plus the official Amharic and Tigray of Ethiopia and Eritrea, respectively. When they fled, they initially went to Egypt, so they spoke Arabic, as well. When they struggled with English in the US, they were working on their fifth language. They counted on every one of the five for their daily existence at some point in their lives. They made endurance before the struggle of serial frustration and embarrassment look easy.

When we learn community languages, we have much less on the line than our friends do with English. We feel sad from the blows to our egos when we sound dumb. Those learning English here bear entirely different risks. While an English speaker can always ask for the English speaker to help them, others may find themselves in dangerous situations because of their non-native English. Abdikadir Abdulahi Mohamed arrived at JFK airport in New York City with a Green Card in late 2017. In spite of his visa and stamp "Admitted-JFK," Customs and Border Patrol (CBP) detained him. "[The CBP interrogator] interrogated me," Mohamed testified, "for 15 hours without a Somali interpreter, even though I asked for one repeatedly." They threatened to deport him, and he could not defend himself because of his lack of fluency in English. In the end, he spent 17 months in detention, incommunicado, even contracting tuberculosis, which will affect his health for the rest of his life.[100]

The interrogators, like the above woman meeting locals, took for granted the complexity and stress of speaking in a foreign language. They incorrectly assumed that it was as easy for him to speak English as it was for them to understand it. Moreover, their grasp of his words led them to believe they understood what he was trying to say. Surely, Mr. Mohamed did not successfully say precisely what he was thinking. One feels full vulnerability speaking a foreign language; adding interrogation by federal agents—likely with no awareness of their linguistic privilege—can make the stress unbearable.

The more you learn the languages of the people in your community, the more you can begin to sympathize with those awkward, embarrassing, brain-bending, precarious situations. An understanding of their difficult daily experience follows. As your experience intersects with theirs, the more you move out of your own point of view—and your view broadens. Empathy brings moral sensitivity and acuity, and you become a more open-minded, caring person.

I love the ego boost I get when I surprise immigrants with my bits of their language, but I know they do not enjoy the reverse. Since folks rarely spend time learning the languages of the community, hearing even poorly executed language often makes them smile with surprise. Americans, however, expect that you speak their language—at home and abroad. If you speak badly, monolingual anglophones often classify you as having "poor" English or substandard "communication skills." Immigrants with an accent may become the target of abuse, and maybe an even bigger target if they appear black or brown. Shame overcomes me when I see such random, impersonal insults after I experienced such praise and admiration for even attempting to speak. The bar is so low for me compared to the standard set for them.

---

[100] "STATEMENT OF ABDIKADIR ABDULAHI MOHAMED* Before the House Committee on the Judiciary: Subcommittee on Immigration and Citizenship," September 26, 2019, https://docs.house.gov/meetings/JU/JU01/20190926/110017/HHRG-116-JU01-20190926-SD012.pdf.

Passive vs. Active Recognition of Differences

Once we have listened to the languages of our community as ecolinguists, learned more about the history of violence done to different languages, and examined what we may take for granted in our daily interactions, we can begin to take positive action. How we engage, though, may not be obvious at first. You can begin by "appreciating" the linguistic landscape, but you would still remain on the other side of the linguistically marginalized. We must engage with those linguistically other people *by our speech* if we want any hope of righting wrongs.

Dr. John Inazu described a way for multiple cultures to live together, which he wrote about in *Confident Pluralism*. As we multiply cultures, and belief systems collide in our country, Inazu seeks a way to allow coexistence among different people. Along the road, we must acquire the ability to live alongside others, in spite of perhaps irreconcilable, deeply held beliefs. He described three "civic aspirations"—tolerance, humility, and patience—that empower this ability.

> *Tolerance* is the recognition that people are for the most part free to pursue their own beliefs and practices, even those beliefs and practices we find morally objectionable. *Humility* takes the further step of recognizing that others will sometimes find our beliefs and practices morally objectionable, and that we can't always "prove" that we are right and they are wrong. *Patience* points toward restraint, persistence, and endurance in our interactions across difference. Importantly, we can pursue these aspirations without agreeing on the reasons for doing so. If enough of us embrace them, we may be able to sustain Confident Pluralism even as we disagree about the underlying justifications.[101]

These aspirations work because they put us in the correct mindset where we realize we do not hold all the answers. Tolerance and

---

[101] John D. Inazu, *Confident Pluralism: Surviving and Thriving through Deep Difference* (Chicago: University of Chicago Press, 2016), 11.

humility both allow us to "recognize," and patience strengthens restraint and endurance.

For example, imagine a family of fundamentalist, Syrian Muslims moves into the house next door who has no interests in my beliefs. They start making unkind comments about the fact that they saw me drink alcohol, and my kids tell me that the mother told them that the only way to get into heaven is by embracing Islam. Furthermore, they hold loud parties in the evening during Ramadan talking and joking in Arabic late into the night, and they terrify my kids when they slaughter a sheep in their backyard during Eid.

We can apply Inazu's approach to this situation. *Tolerance* dictates that I recognize their freedom to practice their religion, and *humility*, that I recognize that they will never agree with my beliefs. *Patience* encourages me to continue to treat them fully as neighbors and fellow humans.

Significantly, all of these aspirations manifest themselves passively. "Recognition" occurs in the mind only; restraint represents a lack of action. Following these ideas will not lead to language-learning and community-bridging success. "Tolerating" differences among languages allows a status quo that kills off different languages, preventing differences from existing. "Humility" simply admits that others might not want to speak my language. "Patience" means we have to keep interacting with these people across language barriers. While these mental exercises and further steps forward will point us in the right direction, they will not change the state of affairs of those who are marginalized.

The relationships between the linguistically different require concrete action on an entirely different path. Learning languages takes us to the next step because it requires dialogue, which by definition cannot be passive. Only persistence and endurance give us the ability to continue to act as we move forward in language and connection. I can practice tolerance, humility, and patience on my side of the fence between us; the action of language requires me to cross it.

We should aspire to action, and learning the languages of our neighbors presents us with the means to succeed actively. Rather than *tolerate* other languages, we let them flow through our own mouths through discipline and hard work. Rather than *humbly* accept differences, we put ourselves in the humbling position of sounding like an ignorant child. Then *patience* takes on a new meaning as we persevere with the daily and weekly actions our language-learning demands.

If I begin to learn Arabic with my hypothetical neighbors, the dynamic changes. I no longer tolerate hearing their language, but I try to speak it. Humility comes when I speak it terribly, allowing myself to be corrected by the children laughing at my mistakes. I exhibit patience as I do not give up in my pursuit of the language. This is the route for me to live as a neighbor, where I hope to hear one day—as one of the boys in Morocco said to me—"You're my brother; you're just not Muslim."

While Inazu teaches us how to live with the divides in our communities, I propose *not* tolerating passively but actively breaching those walls with hard language work buttressed by humility and patience.

Although many people are familiar with the biblical parable of the Good Samaritan, many do not notice that Jesus changed the subject.[102] A lawyer asked a question: "Who is my neighbor?" Jesus responded with the story of a Jewish man who was struck by robbers and left for dead. Two Jewish religious leaders avoided touching the man, while a Samaritan, a mortal enemy of the Jews, picked him up, cleaned him, took him to an inn, and offered his own money to the innkeeper to take care of him.

Mistaking this for the end of the story, people miss the final detail. Jesus next asked the lawyer, "Who was neighbor to that man?" As many teachers do, he changed the question that was actually asked to the one that should have been asked. The question is not who is in what category, but how do I act as I should. I can be humble and patient towards my Syrian neighbors, but I can be a neighbor to them by learning the Arabic language.

---

[102] See Luke 10:25–37.

Vulnerability and Weakness, Growth and Connection

The decision and process of taking on the inherently dangerous work of language-learning initiates an internal change that leads to becoming a more confident, innovative, and creative person as you connect with the local community. I have noticed more discussion about the positive aspects of delving into the areas in our life where we are least comfortable. Anyone who has learned a foreign language has experienced discomfort and even embarrassment. Precisely that dangerous element of vulnerability can transform us into a more creative, compassionate person.

Brené Brown's TED talk demonstrates that becoming vulnerable opens oneself and others up to creativity and dynamism.[103] Dr. Brown says at one point, "Vulnerability is the birthplace of innovation, creativity and change." Most of our life, we run from vulnerability; we hide from shame. This reaction prevents us from being great and courageous, and so by avoiding our weakness, we cannot fully tap into our strengths. When you speak to another with the halting, imperfect, even accidentally insulting words of a foreign language, you enter into a space where you confront your weakness and open yourself to deeper learning.

In the article, "Sure Enough" by Diana Rico, we see that uncertainty fuels knowledge, as doubt releases us from conflict.[104] She describes how confronting her doubt that she can perform a particular yoga pose "gives way to the most delicious feeling of spaciousness in my hip." Once she confronted her doubt in herself, she came into a greater feeling of strength. Rico also presents the results of a study, in which scientists and philosophers identified "uncertainty" as the scientific concept that "would improve everybody's cognitive toolkit." Opening oneself to the fact that one may not be correct–doubt–opens one

---

[103] Brené Brown, *Listening to Shame*, 2012, https://www.ted.com/talks/brene_brown_listening_to_shame.

[104] Diana Rico, "Sure Enough: How Doubt Can Lead to Greater Intimacy, Enhanced Self-Confidence and a Deeper Sense of Spirituality," *Ode*, August 2012, 28–34.

to new knowledge. One who practices doubt with others learns. A language-learner never knows if he or she is saying the right thing, and so becomes a person who is learning constantly.

Peter Blomquist at TEDxRanier describes the way to become more innovative (specifically in the area of global development) by entering into other another culture.[105] He makes three suggestions: 1) Challenge your assumptions. 2) "Zip it"–listen and learn. 3) Accept the hospitality of others. This challenge equals doubt, which allows one to be the learner I mentioned above.

From what I have read, Blomquist is the only one to rank accepting hospitality as an essential trait. I see this trait applies to language-learning as much as the other two. Those who have become fluent in a language have surely spent much time at the table of speakers of that language. By doubting oneself and learning from others, one enters into communion with another; you join together at the table of the other. Much language can be learned when all are open to one another, learning from each other, spending that time together.

I invite you to tap into your strength by confronting weakness and vulnerability. You can become more creative and more innovative, and ultimately move into closer relationships with others. Dr. Brown wrote, "Imperfections are not inadequacies; they are reminders that we're all in this together."[106]

---

[105] Peter Blomquist, "TEDxRanier," *TEDxSeattle* (blog), accessed February 25, 2020, https://tedxseattle.com/talks/peter-blomquist/.

[106] Brené Brown, *The Gifts of Imperfection: Let Go of Who You Think You're Supposed to Be and Embrace Who You Are* (Simon and Schuster, 2010), 61.

CHAPTER 11
200 MISTAKES

Let's take action. If you, my reader, take an action that begins to improve yourself and our society, my writing succeeded. The ideas I present, I intend them as motivation for your next concrete step, not simply as nice things to think about.

The good news is that the first steps are simple. For some, they will be easier than they will be for others. You know the steps. You preformed them before you knew how to walk, before you ever remember. Those steps led you to learn to read and arrive at this day where you can read these words.

Babble. Today.

Make noise. Use one word, or half a word. Say hello—even if you are leaving. When you do not understand what others are saying, change the subject. Ask strangers, "What's that?" in their language. Utter every verb in the present tense—or infinitive, or whatever you happen to remember at the moment.

The only way you can speak a language well is to speak it badly for a long time. Learning a language is like learning how to ice skate. No one takes an ice-skating lesson without standing on the ice. No video or tutoring or podcast about ice skating will make you a good ice skater. You have to skate. And to skate, you must fall. Nowadays, kids learn how to skate with a modified walker to keep them upright. No one would call someone a competent skater if they never graduated from the walker, however. A teenager would rather fall and break their wrist than use a walker.

You cannot avoid badly falling. The more you speak the language badly, the better you will become. The more you embrace your mistakes, the faster is your progress. Contrary to anything your teacher—

or your ego—may have said, the more mistakes you make the better. Benny Lewis, the author of "Fluent in Three Months" and TED speaker, said once that you should make 200 mistakes a day.[107] Can you imagine? That would mean if I am an absolute beginner, I would need to pronounce at least a paragraph 100% wrong before I reached my quota. (This paragraph includes fewer than 200 words.) If I am an advanced beginner, I would have to talk for a few hours—every day, without a break. For a week I would have to make almost 1500 mistakes!

Eventually, you will make more and more glorious mistakes. The beginner skater wipes out when slowly making their way around a curve; a hockey player hits the ice and spins and slides into the boards when making a daring steal. Both of them get back up and keep skating. The beginner language-learner says, "Good morning!" in the evening; the expert uses hopelessly outdated slang. Everyone has a good laugh—and keeps talking.

Enjoy the Bumps in the Road

You go to the store or cafe in another country. You stand in line, repeating your lines in their language, clenching your jaw, hoping you get it right. Someone behind you says something that you do not understand, but you smile and laugh weakly. They do not look happy. Eventually you get to the front of the line. Before you can say your line, the cashier says something fast and furious, which you manage to ignore so you can say what you planned. Then they ask a question. "What?" you reply. Another question comes. People behind you start to talk. Time slows down and you start to sweat. You nod and grimace, agreeing to whatever, hoping to avoid conflict. It is time to pay, and they told you the amount—which you missed. Holding out a handful

---

[107] John Hutchinson and Benny Lewis, "Benny Lewis Reveals How to Learn a Language in Three Months," Daily Mail Online, June 3, 2015, https://www.dailymail.co.uk/travel/travel_news/article-3106032/Speak-like-Tarzan-don-t-embarrassed-aim-make-200-mistakes-day-Irish-polyglot-reveals-learn-language-just-three-months.html.

of change, you let the big—and, you hope, honest—cashier take the right amount so you can run away to cry.

The pressure of speaking a language hurts. Why can we not speak like a child, just opening our mouth and talking? We are adults. People expect responsibility, intelligence, and basic social skills from us. We have to pay for things, stand in line, and clean up after ourselves. No one asks little children important questions because they cannot answer them. People expect us to answer.

Making 200 mistakes a day is hard. The expectations and humiliation and disappointment can overwhelm us. Somehow, we hear and feel anger in the people around us, even though we cannot actually understand the words they are saying.

We expect perfection and place unrealistic expectations on ourselves, and then we place them on the cashiers and other people in line. When we recognize that those mistakes are the *solution* and not the *problem*, the above scenario sounds like success.

My friend told the story of his friend who was determined to speak French. He went to Paris and spoke French with everyone he could. As a result, he often found himself in the very situation I described— but he flipped the script. Rather than sweat and grimace—he laughed loudly and heartily. On multiple occasions, my friend confirmed, whole cafes would be full of laughter. Surely, some folks who thought they were going to drink a simple cup of coffee or buy a loaf of bread brought home a story of the brightest point in their day.

When you learn a community language, you may run across this situation more often than with other languages. In college, my first-year roommate came from Indonesia. I learned a bunch of random words, several about food. Just by pronouncing these words, I could reduce him to clutching his stomach in guffaws. He had never heard an American accent, and his reaction brought everyone in on the delight.

So imagine: you stand in line. You make your way to the front, and after fumbling for words and change—you laugh.

Goal 200

At my work, they take safety very seriously. Zero injuries is the goal. As a result, they post everywhere how many injuries were sustained in the past 100 days. Safety controls exist everywhere, and any associate has the authority to call out violations. If one of the company's associates feels unsafe at a customer or supplier site, they can leave without repercussion from their employer.

Now, you may have been thinking your goal was similar: zero mistakes. To be on the safe side, you have kept your numbers down by not speaking much. Yet, you do not feel confident in speaking. You will need to modify your goal so that you can learn.

Once we set our goal at 200 mistakes per day, we have to completely change our actions. First, we have to find ourselves among speakers of the language. We can find out where those folks hang out, such as a mall or coffee shop. I visited Somali cafes and an Oromo church to find folks to speak to. If we get the opportunity to go to the country, we can solve the problem in one fell swoop.

Second, we have to take the opportunities that we find. That trip to the store—we may make five to ten mistakes in that short exchange with the cashier. Maybe we have to engage those people behind us in line. We can rack up another five to ten mistakes. Such an event can offer us 5-10% of our daily goal.

At that rate, we may not move along quickly enough. We will have to have ten to twenty such conversations. Personally, I cannot shop that much.

One method I saw was to hold a bunch of rote questions in my back pocket. At the store, I can ask in the cereal aisle, "Which one do you like?" or in the produce section, "How do you know which is good?" Just because you know how to find the best peach, or you do not really care which cereal a stranger likes, you can ask nevertheless. I saw a video of someone learning languages walking around the mall in his hometown. He approached someone and asked, "Do you know if this mall has a movie theater?" Of course, he knew. He used the question just so he could follow up, "Oh, do you speak X language?" Then he got to work on his language. You can see in other videos that his conversations concern why he is learning this language and how he did so; so he is always prepared with the correct handful of vocabulary.

"Hi! Do you speak X language?" "Can you help me?" "Do you know how to say Y?" can kick the conversation off. With "I love X language," "My friends taught me X language," "I hope to visit your country one day," and "What city do you come from?" you can continue along. If you memorize the above sentences, or work out different sentences that interest you more, or apply more to the people you are likely to encounter, you will be able to carry on a conversation for several minutes. You will not understand all the responses—that is how you can make it to your mistake goal.

Learning Outside the Classroom

In my late teens I worked as a language conversation partner for university students from Japan. Our goal was simply chat about a subject. I did not grade or even take notes.

One time, a student was speaking to me about work in Japan, and the subject of overwork came up. All of the students had studied English for several years. This student kept bringing up a phrase. His pronunciation was very difficult for me to discern. Other than repeat the phrase, he could not explain himself. Finally, he opened his dictionary (the days before smart phones) and pointed at the word: "softening of the brain." I still had no idea. He took the word from the dictionary but could not pronounce it or explain anything beyond simply showing me the page.

People have different experiences learning languages in a classroom. Class measures their ability with a test. They measure how well you memorize vocabulary that a teacher or book chose as important. Spelling plays an important part. Students also have to memorize grammar rules, and then apply them to a bunch of disembodied sentences, devoid of contexts. Those exercises function like math problems: learn the formula and apply it to get the right answer. Some students pass those tests; others do not.

In either case, people often measure their language ability based on that classroom experience and its tests.

A reality about human language faced that Japanese student: language is not math. Just because you work the "exercise" correctly and come up with the right answer, you may not have solved the problem. In math, you solve the problem and write the answer down. In language, you do not succeed unless the other party grasps your answer. Conversely, in language you can fail utterly at working the "exercise," but if the other person gets it, you succeeded. When those students found the word in the dictionary, they could copy it down on a test and certainly receive a good grade. Since I could not understand it, our conversation came to a standstill. (He still gets credit for a handful of mistakes, though.)

Class will never teach you how to communicate when you do not know the "right" answer. Language-learning requires talking around the topic. If you do not know how to say "hair dryer" you have to say, "Electric thing no water hair. It says, 'BZZZZ!'" If you do not know the conditional tense, you say, "I go to school. Maybe he goes to school and I see him." These phrases will not get you an "A" in class, but they get you through tough conversations.

However, all the classes you took taught you that you had to get it right or you *failed*. Bad grades, red ink, sour looks on the teacher's face all taught you that you were *wrong*. If you were going to learn the language, then you had to learn it right or face shame for your mistakes.

Once you conformed to the teacher's expectations, think about how it paid off for you and your classmates. After I spent the first semester of my high school senior year in France as an exchange student, cut off from English except for a fifteen-minute call to my parents (long-distance was expensive in the 1990s), I came back excited to continue speaking French. In my English class one day, a former student of my teacher came back for a visit. When asked what her major was, she responded, "French." I was so excited that I started speaking French with her right away. I was dreaming of learning languages in college the next year, and I wanted to hear more about her experiences. This girl was flustered by my speaking French, and she bumbled an answer out with a thick American accent. A French major in college simply sounded like one more year of high school French, which did not impress me. After studying French at the same high school as me and specializing in French at the university, she was still unable to carry on a normal conversation with confidence.

Something about my experience put me in a completely different league from a college language major. Thousands of expats prove that simply living in another country does not guarantee fluency. Engaging in—and failing at—speaking French many times a day was the difference. She received direct feedback in the form of graded assignments; my feedback came as real-life responses or requests to clarify. If she got a bad grade, she could sigh and continue to her next class. If I got a bad response, I literally could not move onto my next class or task. I was forced to fail until I got it right. Nothing forced her to get the right answer. Moreover, if I got it wrong, I might get laughs or an adoring look—like you would give to a toddler; if she messed it up, she only got a pitying shake of the teacher's head or that red checkmark. She became an expert at quizzes. I could carry on a conversation because I did so every single day.

You Learn the Language You Speak

In Northern Spain, the population speaks two, completely unrelated languages: Spanish (Castellano) and Basque (Euskara). When you meet someone, that individual may prefer one or the other because of their family or geography. You may prefer the same them or the other one. In either case, each of you can assume that the other will understand you.

This bilingual society poses problems for newcomers, whether they come from another country or even just another region in Spain. Everyone who wants to work must prove that they can pass an exam on the Basque language.

The teacher of the adult Basque education class explained grammar (maybe it was prepositions?) on the day that I sat in. The combination of pronouns and prepositions was baffling. During the break, I asked students about their background. Some came from other parts of Spain for a job, and they needed to take the exam to move ahead. A couple students married Basques and wanted the language to communicate better with their in-laws. Sadly, however, none felt terribly confident in their Basque abilities.

A couple days later, I went out for a walk with the local family we were staying with. As we were sitting in a bar, an African immigrant selling belts walked through. He greeted the people with a smile as he showed them his wares. Our friends remarked with surprise, "He's speaking Spanish and Basque!"

This scene reminded me of young merchants I saw in Marrakech, Morocco. These middle-school aged children worked at their parents' shops, and they hustled to sell to tourists from countries all over Europe. So, as foreigners strolled past, they would greet and bargain with people in French, English, Arabic, and Spanish. When I brought this up with my expat friends, they told me they had heard these boys also bargain in Dutch and Bulgarian. Surely, these children did not learn these languages in school. Their grammar did not sound good, but their languages paid off. They were not considered good at languages but good at sales.

Somehow, the professionals in Basque class were speaking with less confidence than the immigrant merchant. Moreover, the latter learned two languages; the folks in the class spoke Spanish fine. Both wanted to speak the language, and both were motivated, and work motivated both the immigrant and many in the class. The difference: the class itself. One who went out and spoke, could speak. The ones who stayed in class, could not.

When I spoke to my daughter, who is interested in learning and teaching languages, I told her that if teachers want their students to succeed, every test should just measure how long they can hold a conversation with the tools they possess. They can throw grammar and pronunciation out the window. As they speak more, their pronunciation and grammar will improve; if they begin with pronunciation and grammar, they may or may not speak more.

Ego Exhaustion

Mistakes wear on you. Coming up with words—even if they are right—makes our brain hurt. During the first months of living in other countries for more than a month, I found myself sleeping nine hours per day, partially to rest my brain and partially to protect myself from the scorn I perceived from others. Objectively, learning a language challenges us. The blows to the ego and the psychological exhaustion drain us.

Embarrassment strikes at the core of our ego, so be ready when you speak your language, not only from the beginning but well into your advanced stages. Especially in the initial stages, you confuse people. You look full-grown, but sound like a child. Native-speakers talking loudly and slowly with exaggerated expressions occupy a common comedy trope—but this is precisely how we speak with very small children. In fact, you do speak like a child, and you share with small children the frustration of not understanding most of what is going on. (Why do you think kids cry when they do not get what they want?)

Yet you will want to understand what is happening, so you will often respond, "What?" when someone speaks in the language you are learning. They may repeat themselves in the same or similar words. "What?" you respond. They will try again, for your benefit. "Sorry...what?" you say again, with an inelegant apology. After a sigh, or a pitying smile, they might try again. You might grasp a piece, but at some point, one of you may change the subject: "Never mind," with a grimace.

You may have told someone you speak the language before the frustrating, uninformative exchange I just described. Now you might have underwhelmed them by only demonstrating your fluent use of question words. Progress demands moving through these moments of embarrassment to learn at whatever cost.

In spite of the lack of comprehension, you are still exhausted. Parsing through the unfamiliar words and trying to save face take a lot of energy, but without much of a result to show. You feel weak and foolish, like you are panting and wheezing after ascending a single flight of stairs.

This unproductive yet draining experience typifies learning anything from the beginning stages. When I decided to take up swimming, I went to the local pool. I jumped in and started doing laps, but since I was not used to the breathing rhythm, I had to stop every one to two lengths of the pool. After a while, my belly started to hurt, like I was going to throw up, because of the lack of oxygen to my brain. I pushed myself for a long time, until I felt like I got a decent workout. I got out of the pool to go to the showers. The clock showed my workout time: nine measly minutes. After several weeks, I was able to swim for 15 minutes. During these weeks, men and women, young and old, started their workouts before me and ended after me, and I looked more exhausted than any of them. After several months of swimming, though, I could swim for 20-30 minutes without stopping, even varying strokes and turning evenly at the end of the pool, just like everyone around me.

Your first months of conversation may produce just as little communication while leaving you drained—even with a similarly upset stomach from nerves or stress. Listening and computing foreign conversation can leave you depleted, even when you take in so little. My first week as an exchange student in France took place during a holiday. We all sat outside around the table, and people tried to talk to me. After finding out how uninspiring I was, they gave up. They felt like they were talking to a dog: no answers but a head cocked at the occasional familiar word. The conversations, though, still left me tired from the hard work in my head.

Well into my time in Morocco, my friend's mom passed away. I sat at their house, talking and eating all day. I could hold my own for a little while but arrived home with no energy remaining. Then I realized my host dad had just gotten married. They were feasting in the special guest parlor at home. Dutifully, I joined them to eat, drink, and chat. Soon after I arrived, unfortunately, I tried to apologize the best I could, because I could not manage to talk or listen without a growing headache. *Two* such intense social situations laid a burden on me that I could not bear.

These experiences have popped up in many of my languages. I watched films in French, went to a town-hall meeting in Oromo, sat through countless university lectures in Russian, tried to enjoy TV in German. All of them left me spent.

Become Like a Child

"Kids just absorb languages. They're like sponges." Since when do kids learn without effort? It took weeks for my baby to learn how to suck milk from a nipple! My wife worked as a piano teacher, and I saw how much effort it took for a child to learn a song or even a simple rhythm. Kids have to work to learn; it is never free. I do not trust the "just absorb" claim.

As I mentioned in chapter 8, I enrolled my kids in Russian school. But it did not always go easily. Things started off well. They liked the Russian stories that I would read to them at night. My oldest was the first in her class to learn the Cyrillic alphabet. They were the only kids in class with neither a Russian mother nor a Russian father; the rest of the kids had at least one. Nursery rhymes came to their tongues easily. When a little Russian girl came to church one Sunday, my youngest took her under her wing and spoke Russian to her.

Then they got hard: resistance. "Why do we have to speak Russian?" they would holler, occasionally through tears. "It's too hard!" "Can't we just read an English book?" They would try passive-aggression. When I asked a question in Russian, they would avoid my gaze and immediately answer, *Ya ne ponimayu,* "I don't understand." I would slow down and repeat, only to hear more loudly, *Ya. Ne. Ponimayu!* "Russian hour" could easily melt into "wretched hour" with many tears and wailing.

I learned that children could learn a language, but that they needed a community, not a class, because it was just as difficult for their brains as for an adult. If they had to "perform" Russian it would not work. Their brains were brutally utilitarian; if they could get by with one word for "water," they would not learn another. Knowing that I spoke English and would do so once Russian hour was over, caused them to suffer through avoiding the difficult cognitive task of learning another language.

For this reason, immigrants require the support of a community for their children to learn their language in addition to English. The American Russian-speaking friends, whom I introduced in chapter 3, constructed their own little community. Mama, "Baba" ("Grandma"), and four kids sufficed, as Mom carried out all conversation in Russian.

I saw the results. When their oldest was three, she did not speak much. I would talk to her and she would barely respond. Then one time, I spoke to her in Russian and she began to chatter delightfully. It was not that she could not speak; she spoke Russian better than English.

Was it easy for these children to speak both languages? Once I was talking with her monolingual, English-speaking father. One of the children, about three or four years old, pled with me in her hybrid language, "Speak *po-russki* (in Russian)*!* Speak *po-russki!*" Having to listen to me speak English was surely making her head tired!

Every language-learning method informs you that *their* method allows you to learn as a child would, but it begs the question of how children actually learn language. Let us begin with the most easily observed facts about children's learning:

They are selfish.

They only care about what they care about, and not what you care about. If they are hungry, they want to eat now. They cannot comprehend how "convenient" it might be for you. If they are tired, they will lie down: in a grocery store, on the ground at the zoo, or under a church pew. If they need something, they will make sure you know. If you do not understand, that is your problem. They do not negotiate.

They do not understand social norms, only emotion. So, if it is inappropriate to lie down on a sidewalk, they do not care. If you become angry, they may get scared—but that will not prevent them from crying. If you try to correct them, they may or may not feel like doing what you want. If they start to cry, you likely cannot make them stop. When you talk to them, they may or may not pay attention. Should they not understand what you are saying, they very well may simply change the subject to something they enjoy talking about.

If you, therefore, want to learn like a child, you can learn a few things from their approach. First, ignore embarrassment. You will make mistakes, be misunderstood, and sound like a fool; make peace with it. Second, speak like your life depends on it. Others can sort through your word-salad to make sense of what they can. Third, feel free to change the subject. You can talk about what you want.

Since you are an adult, you can employ some social graces as you engage these ideas. Social grace and cuteness separate adults and small children. Little kids are adorable, and adults less so, so we need to make up for that difference with social intelligence. You can apologize, explain that you love their language and want to learn more, and beg that others help you with a particular topic that is dear to you.

Prepare yourself for some strange emotions as you enter into these conversations and relationships. Frustration has probably already come up. The pain of isolation strikes hard as we pour our effort vainly into connecting with others, and our attempts fall flat. When we feel that all our work is not paying off, we often feel sad because of everything else we could have been doing with our time.

Ultimately, children are vulnerable. Their life depends on adults, and they have to trust that adults will give them what they need.

Your pursuit is honorable, but your position is vulnerable. Feel your emotions, knowing that all of us picking up this arduous, joyful task of language-learning feel them, too. That discomfort reminds you that you are still moving along on the road of learning. As Brené Brown said, "Staying vulnerable is a risk we have to take if we want to experience connection."[108]

"I'd like to thank everyone for learning English."

I began with this phrase in German as I addressed my audience at an academic conference in Mainz, Germany, and continued, "so I can read my paper in English." I wanted to start my paper with a brief joke as I read the rest in my native language.

After the paper, a Dutch colleague approached me with a response. "Thank you for saying that," he expressed earnestly. "We've never heard an American say anything like that." He embarrassed me; I meant it as a joke. I had not intended such a sincere, earnest statement.

I often hear more internationally-minded Americans praise Europeans, "They all know like three to four languages. You just drive a few hours and there you are in a new country with a different language. Europeans are lucky!" This "luck," though, rests on two unexamined assumptions.

First, while Europeans can drive a few hours to a new country for another language, I can drive 20 minutes and find myself in a majority Somali, Spanish, or Hmong neighborhood. So many people consider the US a monolingual country, but hundreds of languages are spoken in all of our metropolitan areas. Even out in rural parts of the US, one can not only find Spanish in Fremont, Nebraska, but also Lingala in Springfield, Missouri, Ojibwe in Bemidji, Minnesota, and Kunama in Sioux Falls, Iowa. Since we know that Americans very rarely learn these languages, proximity to other languages clearly does not necessary lead to learning them.

Second, Europeans do not come out of the womb multilingual; they work for it, as my Dutch colleague reminded me. Most Germans, Swedes, and Norwegians start learning English in school at age nine; many watch TV and movies in English with subtitles in their own

[108] Brené Brown, *The Gifts of Imperfection: Let Go of Who You Think You're Supposed to Be and Embrace Who You Are* (Simon and Schuster, 2010), 53.

language. It is common for students to take a gap year after high school to study abroad in the US or UK to perfect their language. They likewise spend less time playing sports or participating in other extra-curricular activities, unless they plan to pursue them professionally. Thus, much of the time US kids spend on activities, Europeans spend learning English. Moreover, leisure time is permeated by English. In Macedonia, the quality of the translation of *Harry Potter: The Sorcerer's Stone* into Macedonian was considered poor. It went out of print because reading it in the original English was a better alternative. Since kids wanted in on this worldwide Harry Potter phenomenon, they worked hard at their English to read a full-length novel.

When I thanked my colleagues, I—albeit unknowingly—was recognizing their hard work. They did not simply "speak" English; they *learned* English by *studying* it. While my fluency in English allowed me to choose to read my paper in my native language, they did not possess this privilege. He could not read in his native Dutch, but had to read in a foreign language. When introducing myself in German got too hard for me, I could just stop and revert to English without embarrassment; he pushed through in English without thinking.

It reminded me that whenever I hear someone speaking English with an accent, there is hard work behind that so-called "defective" speech. People who assume people are "born" speaking other languages do not know the work that people have to put into it.

Even If You Sound Dumb

An experience several years ago reminded me that a failure at language can be a gain for everyone. I put my money where my mouth was, and I went down to my Iranian neighbors' house to chat. Since it was the Muslim festival of Eid al-Fitr, I made some cookies to bring down to them, and I brought my wife. I needed some kind of excuse to go visit; I was not brave enough to go "just like that."

Real life differs from language classes. In language classes, speaking wrong results in failure. If I forget my vocabulary, spelling, or grammar, I get marked down. Imagine if I could get credit in language class simply because I came and spoke some of that language, no matter how flawed? In reality, when I speak languages with folks, the latter is certainly the case. My failure is rewarded and prompts me to improve.

When I went to the neighbors' house, I learned two things. When I declared, "Eid mubarak!" ("Blessed Eid!"), they gave me puzzled looks. I immediately learned that they are not Muslim as I assumed. They are Baha'i. The wife's family has been Baha'i for multiple generations, and the husband is half-Muslim and half-Baha'i. He professes to be Baha'i, though.

I started fretting inside myself, hoping I did not offend them. I know that the Baha'i in Iran have occasionally endured persecution. How does it feel for others to assume you are their oppressors? Probably not good. Would Russian Jews be happy to be wished, "Happy Easter!" considering Holy Week historically was a typical time for pogroms? Not likely. I felt pretty uncomfortable wishing my Baha'i neighbors blessings on this Muslim holiday.

Second, I learned my Farsi is no less awkward than my familiarity with my neighbors' religion. I was able to form questions but was unable to understand responses. My wife–who does *not* know Farsi–even interpreted their questions for me somehow when I could not understand them. I could barely get out my house number "one-six-one-three." At least I nailed "I don't understand"! My Farsi seemed to complicate the situation, which made me even more uncomfortable.

So, how did they react? They kissed me and my wife. The husband grabbed the back of my neck and pulled me in and kissed both cheeks. The wife did the same with my wife. Their adult daughter held my wife's hand and would not let go. This kiss came as a result of my failure. Unlike language class, reality showed my failure was a success. They showed that while my gut said "fail," the reality was "gain."

Setting up your 200-mistakes environment enables you to fail fast and often, through all the completely opaque things you stumble to express, all the unfunny jokes you try to tell, and all the hilarious things you say on accident. As the blows to the ego assault you, you can empathize with the people around you struggling to use your language day-in and day-out to make their living and get through the day. Learning community languages means that you have to speak a language you know badly to people who have to navigate their lives in a language not native to them.

We do not need to worry about failing when we focus on other people. Stumbling on cultural and linguistic matters *helps* the situation, when we focus on relationships. At times we need information, so confusion seems like a failure. If I had a business or legal deal with this family, things would have been difficult (impossible?) because so much information would have been lost. However, the fact that I went in for the relationship first, the situation ended beautifully. If I needed to do business with them at this point, I know that now things would go smoothly. They think of me and my family as good people, as good neighbors who make an effort to know them, their culture, and language. Effort clearly trumps failure in the long run.

Fail and accept the kiss of appreciation.

CHAPTER 12
START TODAY

Loving one's neighbor, establishing a more welcoming atmosphere, pluralism—all of these swim in my head as abstractions. I cannot always tell if I am helping these goals though my actions because the outcome looks different to each person. Sometimes I fool myself into thinking that I am doing them, but then someone informs me that, in fact, I am not doing so.

If I am speaking another language, the action is unambiguous. No one can say that I am not speaking the language (though, of course, people can say that I am not doing so *well*, which is a different question). This book draws the direct line from speaking the language of your neighbors—to whatever degree you can—to pluralism that includes everyone, welcoming others, and love towards our neighbors.

This chapter will guide your next steps. You can repeat them as many times as necessary in whatever way works for you.

Your Neighbor is Your Teacher

When I practiced my languages overseas, this truth permeated my mind. "I'm going to sound dumb to anyone in earshot as soon as I open my mouth." Keeping my mouth shut clearly did not teach me anything. Flipping my point of view, though, revealed a boundless classroom. I might sound dumb, but since everyone in my line of sight knows more than me, I can take advantage and learn.

See your neighbors as teachers—right at home. Historically, the offspring of immigrants view other immigrants and indigenous people as threats. We have attempted to solve this problem through two approaches: restrict immigrants and indigenous to their occupations and land, and force those in our midst to act and talk like us. To think of these human beings as teachers flips the script.

Language changes the power script. Rather than centering the dialogue on monolingual anglophones, we move the anglophones to the margin. While we anglophones are speaking that other language, we no longer are teaching them how to live and act like us; they teach us.

The teaching and learning activities are clear and concrete. When you hear someone speak another language, engage. If you find yourself at the airport, notice the languages. At your favorite restaurant, ask if your server speaks a language—or multiple languages—other than English. Waiting in line at the grocery store, greet the people in front and in back of you in line.

Ask how to say a word—even one single word. Take the opportunity for a lesson.

Or, if you learned a few words already, take the opportunity for a "quiz." Address the person in their language and see if you get it right—or if you at least get a smile. Whether you succeed or fail, do so gracefully.

You can ask whatever you want, talk about what you want. After I noticed lots of Ethiopians working at the places I frequented, I learned how to say in Amharic, "Hello! How's work?" I always get a smile and an answer in Amharic. When the internet technician came to check my connection, I asked him how to say "plug in" in Spanish.

If you ask a person how to say, "Hello! How are you?" you may find that the next time you get the opportunity to use it, you forgot. Nothing is stopping you from asking the next person how you say the same things. You can ask ten or more times. It does not matter: the person you are asking now does not know how many times you may have already asked in the past.

Please remember how little accuracy matters. You are a beginner, a child in an adult body. The other person holds the knowledge. You do not need to fool anyone. I asked one person for a phrase, wrote it down on a card, and then literally read the greeting off that notecard, only to receive a blank look because I still did not say it right. The person figured out what I was trying to say and corrected me, so I could correct my card and my pronunciation—for the next time. We always work it out—together.

Give up Your Privilege

In the discussions I hear about privilege, people lament the inequity. I agree that those of us who hold privilege cannot too easily accept the current state. At the same time, we have to admit that the privilege— some "haves" alongside a majority of "have-nots"—is the current state of affairs. We need to take a step forward now, this week if not today.

If you are reading this book, you know English. You bear linguistic privilege, which I detailed above. How do we create more "haves" from among the "have-nots"?

Many have assumed the solution is to teach English to more people. They consider this an act of kindness and charity to others, and well-meaning English-speakers even volunteer so as to take on the burden themselves rather than place it on the one needing help with English. The English students, once they have acquired this new language, gain access to new jobs and media where more material prosperity lies.

The student, however, must take on a large burden in this scenario. As I mentioned above, they must confront a world hostile to those who speak English badly—not a good environment to practice in. Because of their lack of fluent English, they are likely working strenuous, physical jobs, so studying and practicing after work and on weekends adds to the exhaustion. Becoming a "have" comes at the expense of spending time with family or relaxing. So, while the teacher offers something to the student—for money or for free—but the student always pays in time and often in further difficulties.

The question itself that I raised begs the question of what each one has or does not have. For those with ears to hear, the non-English speaker possesses at least one other language. If we contrast the "have" with the "have-not," we can say that the monolingual English-speaker lacks other languages, while the non-English speaker possesses another language, thus turning the have/have-not categories upside-down.

Thus, by valuing the language that every individual speaks, we reevaluate haves vs. have-nots. Those who speak a language other than English is a "have" compared to us. We work to acquire it so that *we* can be transformed from have-not to have. Their language makes them wealthy.

Ultimately, the burden shifts, as well. Rather than sit the non-English-speaker in our class, we sit in theirs. We memorize, we work, and—most importantly—we take on the vulnerability of sounding dumb. Rather than putting in our effort so that another can change, we change ourselves. We shift our point of view, humbling ourselves, so that we value what others possess and so that we become open and willing to learn.

Just Start

You do not have to follow any method; feel free to turn to classes, tutors, and various teaching methods, or apps, videos, and books. Use all the resources you can find, but do not spend more time than you must looking for the resources. In learning Oromo, a woman with a paper notebook and constant contact at work with native Oromo-speakers made much faster progress than I did with my electronic notebook, flashcard app, and PhD. Be practical.

Remember, though, these basic assumptions.

1. Your neighbor holds something precious, which society or even your neighbor might undervalue.

2. Your neighbor is the richest, most complete resource that you will find for the language.

3. Language is about communication and relationships. You learn languages through communication and relationships. The result is communication and relationships.

4. By humbling yourself, you will connect more deeply with your neighbor. By learning their language, you will humble yourself and connect more deeply with your neighbor.

By following these notions, you will connect with something deep inside you, learning languages the way your ancestors did for a hundred generations, the way millions of people do till the present day. Setting your device down, you will stumble through vulnerable moments and see the twinkle in your neighbor's eye as they see you smile in your success.

www.ingramcontent.com/pod-product-compliance
Lightning Source LLC
Chambersburg PA
CBHW070039100426
42740CB00013B/2733